FINDING JOY

A DOG'S TALE

DANIELA AMATO

ILLUMIFY MEDIA GLOBAL
Littleton, Colorado

Published by
Illumify Media Global
www.IllumifyMedia.com
"We bring your book to life!"

Library of Congress Control Number: 2020920917

Paperback ISBN: 978-1-947360-72-3
eBook ISBN: 978-1-947360-73-0

Typeset by Art Innovations (http://artinnovations.in/)
Cover design by Debbie Lewis

Printed in the United States of America

CONTENTS

To my children, Anthony and Marisa. I love you both unconditionally and endlessly.

ACKNOWLEDGMENTS

To Ivan Whittenburg – Thank you for your encouragement and help in this emotional process!

To Growl Rescue, Jordan Koch, and everyone else involved in rescuing Little Bear and countless others.

To Little Bear – You were, and continue to be, my greatest teacher of Life and Life's true meaning.

To Universe, Life Source, God, Spirit – none of this would be possible without your Divine guidance.

Everything has a purpose. Some beings know instinctively; others, it takes time and searching. The journey is not always easy. Yet, when your purpose becomes clear it is the most incredible, joyful, fulfilling, and amazing experience!
I hope everyone finds their purpose.
Cheers!

PREFACE

I want to share my story with you. It may seem strange to you that I, a dog, have the desire to share my story with the world. It is not strange, however. Every being has a need to be heard, to be seen, and to make a difference. I think you will see why my story is important for everyone involved. Some parts of my story are a little cloudy. Other parts are so vivid it is as if I am reliving it now!

I have had many names over the years, but this story is about my life as Little Bear. I am, or was, a seventeen–pound terrier mix. My human thought I was the cutest thing in the world, and honestly, I agree. My best feature, according to every human who ever saw me, were my eyes. Soulful eyes, they were called. "The eyes are the windows to the soul," someone said. My soul has lived through many lives. I have seen a lot. I guess hints of this shine through my eyes and penetrate anyone who looks directly at them. I like to think it is a super-power. I can hypnotize or melt anyone who looks at me. I don't, though. I just let them see what they can, and that is usually *love*.

This story begins in 2009. I will make references to years prior along the way because some things carry forward and are important. All my lives and experiences have led to a moment in

August 2019. It is a great story—a great life. Seatbelts on! This is a road trip like no other! I hope you enjoy my story, and I hope, in some way, it will help you understand your purpose.

As my mommy says . . .

One Love.

FALLING

I was falling. I felt like I was gliding down a liquid slide, swirling around the atmosphere in a ball of light. The slide was dark with purple ribbons flowing through it. I could not feel it, but I had the sense that it was silky and smooth, like a beautiful silk ribbon. The sides were slightly raised to keep from falling off. The wind blew gently, helping the ribbon turn and twist through the air.

I do not know how long or fast I glided. I could not see anything outside the slide. There were streaks of lights and sparkles, and I had the sense that there were other souls here with me. A low gentle hum accompanied me on this slide. It was not scary at all. It was exciting. The glide was pointing down, and it seemed that the farther along I went, the faster I slid. The air changed slightly. A little heavier. Denser. My excitement grew. This was going to be an interesting adventure!

With a sudden thrust off the side of the slide, I was propelled forward until I was pushed through a thin, warm barrier. I landed with a gentle plop inside a little vessel that was inside a larger one. It did not hurt at all. I heard a rhythmic beat pulsing all around me and sounds I could best describe as a rippling stream. The beat and the rippling sounds were comforting, and I felt a gentle motion that resembled rocking.

It was dark in here, with occasional strings of light shooting past. My little vessel had found a spot along the wall and attached to it. It was now plugged into the power source. It felt good and safe here.

I had just completed the first stage of my journey.

There were several other souls in here with me. I was not alone. All the others were also attached to the power source. I think they arrived before me; not by long, but they seemed more settled and positioned along the wall of the power source. Our vessels sometimes moved, swaying back and forth, but they always stayed attached to the power source. We huddled together and listened to the beating sounds and rippling stream of our new home. I would soon understand that the power source was my mother. She was our reason for being and gave us the strength and nourishment we needed to grow.

The next two months we spent together relaxing, sleeping, and feeling full. We started changing inside here. Growing. I felt happy and fell asleep often, waking up on occasion to move around and get more comfortable. Sometimes, the beat would speed up and the gentle rocking felt more like bouncing. I was able to hear sounds outside of mother, although the sounds were muffled. I noticed the beat was faster when sounds felt angry. I did not like this very much, so I would try to move closer to the other souls. When the angry feeling passed, the beat relaxed. Our mother sent us messages:

"I love you," "I'll protect you," "Remember always that I love you."

These messages were subtle. We felt them in her heartbeat. We felt them inside us, like a warm blanket wrapped around us. We sent her messages too. This was a good place. It was beginning to feel very crowded though.

Our bodies grew legs, a head, and a tail. The legs of the others kept kicking me. I tried to keep mine close to me so as not to annoy them. The others were not as considerate. They were bigger than me, and I often felt legs pushed in my face and body. My legs were not as big; mine seemed shorter. I wished the others would move over to give me more room. One of the others wiggled close to me. This one seemed gentler than the rest. It was nice to huddle with someone who was not kicking and shoving. The two of us stayed close together for the remainder of our time in here, only wiggling to avoid a foot or shoulder in our faces.

2

BIRTH

*S*omething was changing. A force was pushing us with rhythmic, pulsing squeezes. The heartbeat moved faster and louder. The others moved on top of each other, and I was squashed and kicked. There was something familiar about this. I had done this before. I told myself to stay calm. I tried to tell the others to stay calm too, but they were panicking and moving frantically. I slipped behind everyone, not on purpose, but only because the others pushed me out their way. It was fine. I stayed back and hung onto the power source for as long as I could. It would be what was meant to be.

The others led the way. One by one, we were pulled off the power source and squeezed at the same time. I held onto someone's tail with my mouth. I think it belonged to the gentle soul. *Stay calm. Stay calm*, I repeated to myself. The heartbeat slowed down for a moment or so, giving me time to gather my thoughts. There was more room to move around now. Maybe I would be able to stay in here with my friend. I yawned and let go of the other's tail. My friend slipped away, and now I was alone. Suddenly, there was a big push from behind me. The heartbeat sped up, and I was drawn into a tight passage. I tried to make myself smaller, so I did not get too squashed. There was another shove and I fell through onto a hard surface.

I felt so cold. It felt strange being here outside of the warmth. I heard many sounds but not the heartbeat. No sound of the running stream. No rocking. There was only hardness and cold. I began to panic. *What do I do?* I opened my mouth and air rushed into my body. I swallowed the air. Okay. I understood. I must work to breathe now. The air hurt my lungs a little at first. After a few breaths, it was okay.

The others were there making little noises. I had never heard them before. I tried to make the same sound. Mine sounded softer and higher pitched. We all huddled together; we were all crying and trying to swim like we did for the past two months, but nothing happened. After a few moments, the others started wiggling away, doing the swimming motion but slightly different. They were moving together as a group. I could not see. None of us could. Light came through our eyelids though, and we could see slight shadows of things. Without sight, we relied on smell to guide us. I was able to smell the others and suddenly smelled Mom, too. I searched for the gentle one. When I found her, I followed her and stayed close.

The other souls were not only bigger but also stronger. They wiggled to Mom's belly first and latched on to a plug on the outside of her. They made funny slurping sounds. They were eating and doing so ravenously. I tried to wait my turn, but I felt so hungry. Wiggling and squirming, I figured out how to get in between everyone, and they barely noticed me because I was so small. When one let go of the power source, Mom's teat, I grabbed it. It was soft and warm and dripping with milk. I latched on and began to make slurping sounds just like the others. Hm, so delicious! I heard the heartbeat while I drank. It sounded different out here, but I knew it was the same heartbeat; this was my mom, my power source, my life giver. It was comforting to hear her. While I drank, Mom was cleaning all of us. Her tongue felt rough but gentle. She did a great job cleaning us. I wasn't scared anymore. I was content. Happy, even. I was outside with my mom and the others. We all stayed together in a pile. That kept us warm.

Little by little our bodies changed. One day, my eyes opened! I did it slowly because my eyelids felt stuck together, and I did not want to hurt myself. My eyes were wet and dripping with a sticky-feeling water. Mom licked our faces until our eyes were fully opened and clear. I could see everything around me! Everything looked so big. Things had different shapes to them and carried different smells. For example, the trees each had their own scent. This scent was different from the grass, different from bushes, and different from each other. Everything had a unique smell. My nose twitched quickly to smell everything. With my eyes newly opened, I was able to associate smells to what I saw. This was very exciting, indeed!

The next few weeks we spent huddled together, eating, and getting cleaned by Mom. We learned to stand, walk, and relieve ourselves. Mom rarely left us alone. Sometimes she got up to relieve herself or eat. I noticed she did not eat the same way we did. She ate from a bowl and used teeth to chew. I moved my tongue in my mouth and noticed I didn't have teeth. I wondered when I would get them. Her ears were always pointed in our direction, and if one of us made a sound, she would stop and turn toward us to make sure we were okay. When she came back to us, I could smell the food she ate. It smelled different from her milk.

There were also different sounds. The wind carried messages from things far away. The messages from the trees and other creatures were most active in the quiet parts of the day, but you could always hear something. Insects, for example, never stopped talking. It was fun to put everything together. I paid special attention to everything. Nature has messages to help us and guide us. Other noises were not from nature; they were horrible sounds: loud, abrasive, negative sounds. I did not like them at all but felt I had to pay attention to them as well. Sometimes, when the noises became too much, I found comfort lying near my Mom, next to her heart, listening to her heartbeat. That was my favorite sound in the world.

My sibling souls were still much larger than me. They were bigger and faster and stronger. I tried to keep up with them because I wanted to play. I tried and tried, but it was difficult for me. Mom would bark at me calling me to her. I bounced back to her and drank from her teat while she cleaned me.

I heard her say, "That's okay. Take this time to drink more. That will help you grow big and strong."

She was very kind to all of us. When the others pushed me around, she did not jump in right away. She wanted me to learn how to fight for myself. Sometimes, the others got too rough and knocked me down hard. Mom did not like that and sent a low growl. They stopped right away. One of my sibling souls stayed close to me. She was bigger than me, but she was not pushy. I knew right away who she was! She was my friend from inside the warm place. She was the one whose tail I held. She was the one who kept close to me for comfort. I decided to help her get to Mom for food when the others were blocking her way. I watched out for her. When the others pushed her around, I made a low growl sound mimicking the growl Mom made. They listened! I must have sounded very scary for them to listen. I felt proud and more confident. I became the protector of this sibling soul, and we became best friends.

There were other beings around us all the time. They were two–legged beings. It seemed like they were covered in a dark cloak. They talked loudly and were not gentle. They were rough with Mom and yelled at her a lot. When they gave her food, they threw the bowl down so that it made a loud noise. She ate her food eagerly but looked up nervously at them. Mom was always on guard around them. I did not like the two–legged creatures. They made me nervous.

One day, the two–legged creatures were talking loudly near all of us. Mom started barking at them. She was asking them to be quiet. Instead, they threw a rock in our direction. It hit Mom on her back leg, causing her to yelp. The two-legged creatures laughed a weird sound. It was not a happy sound. It had an uncomfortable feeling about it. Mom made low throat sounds at us telling us to move closer to her. We gathered around her and she kept us warm and out of sight of those strange beings. Mom never took her eyes off them. I wondered if Mom ever got any rest.

She sent us messages. "I love you," "Learn well the lessons of nature," "Remember who you are," "I love you." Mom repeated "I love you" over and over. It was as if she wanted to make sure we never forgot. Love is the most important message, after all.

Something seemed different about Mom. She felt tense. Mom was worried about something. I tried to figure it out but fell asleep with Mom's milk dribbling out of my mouth. How embarrassing.

3

TRUCKS

*I*t was nighttime. I could tell because there were fewer noises and the sky was dark. We were all huddled together with Mom. We were settling down and getting comfortable for sleep. There was something different about this night. I twitched my nose in the air and felt something uncomfortable. The air felt tense. Mom scooped us closer to her with her legs. She felt the tension too. We drifted off to sleep until we felt Mom lift her head quickly. Her ears were straight up listening for something. That something came in the form of heavy thumping. The thumping was the boots of one of the two–legged creatures. He had a smell on him that made me nervous.

One by one he picked us up. We all whined and tried to stay close to Mom. Mom barked and showed her teeth. He ignored her and pushed her head to the side. One by one, he dropped us into a box. We all started crying, and Mom was barking. Mom had different barks. Some of them were greetings, friendly and warm. Others were warning barks, telling someone to stay away or warning us of danger. Tonight, Mom's bark was upset and scared. She was telling them to bring us back. She was calling to us to come to her. We tried to get out of the box, but it was too tall. I could barely see over the top, but it was enough to see Mom leaping forward to run to us; something around her neck yanked her back, and she fell backwards. Mom tried again and again. Each time she was pulled back, and she cried in pain and fear. Then Mom's bark changed a little.

Now she was barking at us, crying out, saying "I love you all! Be careful! Trust your instincts! Be happy!"

My best friend and I cuddled together closely. We were scared. We were all scared. Even the bigger ones were scared and confused. The two–legged creature picked up the box and walked away from Mom. Mom stopped barking and lay down, defeated; I heard her crying. We all cried too.

We were carried in this box and put inside another box. A metal door slammed shut loudly. I could hear Mom outside, barking and crying. We all answered her with our own cries. Mom. I wanted Mom. The bigger box started moving. The motion rocked us to sleep as we huddled together. I did not sleep well. I kept waking up hoping to be near Mom. The box smelled dirty and bad. Where were we going? Why wasn't Mom with us? When the big box stopped, the two–legged creature took us out and put us back on the ground in our box. We all called out hoping Mom would hear us. From inside the box, we could not see where we were. I stuck my nose up to smell the air. This was not where we lived with Mom. This place was different.

It was chilly out. There were lights, but not from the sky. The lights came from tall metal structures and shone too brightly, and yet not brightly enough. There were loud noises coming from other huge moving metal boxes. The ground shook as they passed us by bringing a gust of wind that made us all shiver. We cuddled closer together. Crying and yelping, we called out in hopes that Mom would hear us and come for us. I do not know how long we stayed here. It seemed like an awfully long time. Some of the others fell asleep for a little while. When they woke up, they called out to Mom again. I never stopped calling for her. I called her with my mind and my voice and begged her to come to us. She never did.

I heard Mom's voice inside my head. "I'm sorry. I cannot come. I love you." We never saw Mom again.

4

_____

RESCUED

*C*rying, hungry, cold, and wet from rain, we remained in this box for a long time. We relieved ourselves in the box, and that became uncomfortable and gross. We climbed on each other and tried to stay warm. I went to a corner of the box and lay my head down. My friend came over and lay her head down next to me. She stuck her tongue out and licked my face. I did the same to her. At least we had each other. The bigger ones were just as scared. I realized in that moment that size does not matter. Fear is fear; sadness is sadness.

I tried to be brave for my best friend. I pretended I was not scared and that made me feel a little braver. It seemed to help her knowing I was close, knowing I was not scared. I looked over the box edge by standing on my back legs, like a two–legged creature. I was not able to clear the top, but I was able to see more. I understood why they moved around like that. The view of things far away was much better in this position. There wasn't a lot to see; no trees, no grass, just hard roads, and a lot of metal moving boxes. I sat down and curled up next to my friend. *It would be okay*, I told myself. It would be what was meant to be.

A moving metal box pulled up close to us. A two–legged female came out. She was not covered in a dark cloak like the other two–legged creatures. She had an illuminating golden globe all around her; it appeared as though she radiated bright-ness, like the moon or sun. Her voice was kind and sweet, her eyes the same. We looked up at her from our box. At first, we were silent, unsure of what to expect; once we heard her voice, we began making sounds in return. We yelped and whined and squirmed around each other. Maybe she would bring us to our mom.

The golden two–legged creature lifted our box off the ground and put it in her metal box. It smelled different from that stinky metal box that dumped us here all alone. This metal box smelled nice, like flowers. She talked to us the whole time we were moving. I watched her carefully. The others were crying and squirming, but I remained still and watched her every move-ment and gesture. When she moved her mouth, sounds came out that were not moans or groans or barks like we made. The sounds were different, but I could tell she was sending us calm messages. She spoke like the other two–legged creatures, but her sounds were not angry and hateful. They were kind and loving. I decided to listen closely to her sounds and watch her move-ments. I had the sense that I needed to learn from her and her messages.

I think I fell asleep. I was still sitting, but I was sleeping. Odd. I hoped the others did not see that.

We were not in the box anymore, not the metal box and not our box. We were not outside. It appeared to be a huge box-like structure that kept out the sun, wind, air, and pretty much everything. Everything was hard and cold and smelled funny. There were more two–legged creatures moving all around us. They were kind. They were petting us and looking at our faces closely. They fed us from a teat that was not at all like Mom's. This one was hard and had a funny taste to it. The milk was good, even though it was not like Mom's milk. We were all so hungry that we took the fake teat with fake milk eagerly. We ate and I fell asleep again, this time curled up next to my friend. We spent several days here. We were poked and fed and poked some more. They kept us in a small box that had openings on the sides where I could fit my paw. We were all together, which was nice. My friend stayed especially close to me. I had to be brave for her. I had to be brave for all of us. Mostly, I had to be brave for me.

Time moves differently for dogs. I think I should explain that now. Every moment is a new and separate moment. We constantly adjust to each moment, greeting it with either joy or hesitation, depending on what we smell in the air around us. We can tell if another being is good or bad. We can feel things through our paws on the ground. We hear things from extremely far away. All of this helps us decide what the new moment will bring. This keeps things interesting and new. This also means that the space between good things seems so far apart.

Our time with Mom seemed like a lifetime ago. It was over. Our life with Mom was no more. Yet, I know that if I ever saw Mom again, it would be the happiest occasion ever. We never forget the good. We never forget our family. Nothing can erase that from our memories. Nothing or no one.

I was obsessed with learning things. I watched everything and everyone. I smelled everything and licked everything my tongue could reach. I learned that two–legged creatures were called humans. My other sibling-souls were my littermates. We were puppies until we got older and then would be called dogs. This place where we were now was called a veterinary hospital or the Vet for short. They took care of all kinds of animals there. We were going to stay there until a family wanted us or until they ran out of room. Then, if there was no more room for us, they would "put us to sleep." I did not like the humans' faces when they said that. Something seemed very wrong about that. I hoped there would be a family for us soon. I also discovered that my littermates and I were only a few weeks old. The doctor said that it was too soon to be away from Mom, and that is why we were given the pretend teat and pretend milk all the time. Of course it was too soon to be away from Mom. I knew that. We all did.

The funniest thing I learned was that when humans showed their teeth, they were not angry or trying to be tough. They were happy. What a weird way to express happiness! I supposed that was because humans do not have tails to wag. Poor things.

I also discovered humans do not have fur. They just have skin. How ridiculous is that? It did not make any sense to be without fur. No wonder they could not keep warm and must put other things on their body to get warm. Some of the things were nice. For example, the doctor had a soft, warm cloth in our cage. It was extremely comfortable and kept the cold from the metal away from us. I liked to pretend that I was making a den by moving the material around with my nose and paws. Then, when I thought it was ready, I would get in the middle and lie down. This seemed to amuse the humans. They wondered how I knew to do that at such a young age. This was confusing to me. I thought everyone knew these things. Then I remembered something Mom said as we were being taken away. She said, "Trust your instincts." *Instincts*. Making the den must be one of those instincts. I rested my head on my paws and thought about this some more. "Thank you, Mom, for giving me good instincts." I hoped Mom could hear me.

I wanted to run around and play. I was tired of being in this cage. I tilted my head back and let out a sound that was straight from my belly. The humans put their hands together and said, "He howled! Oh, the little dear!" and they showed their teeth.

Howling. I seemed to remember the feeling of howling. It felt good. It felt ancient. It felt like my heart was coming out through my mouth in a beautiful sound. My other littermates just looked at me. They tried to howl, but my howl was the best–sounding of all of them! My friend told me that too. This made me incredibly happy.

5

BEAR

We were loaded back into a metal box, which I learned was called a car. This car also smelled nice but had the scents of other dogs that came before us. I wondered where they went. I wondered where we were going. It seemed we were always going somewhere. I took my usual spot in the corner of the box next to my friend. We liked to stay close to each other. It gave us comfort. We licked each other's faces and then settled down for the ride.

The drive in the car was pleasant, except for when the bigger cars, called trucks, drove by. I hated them. They reminded me of being taken away from Mom and being left outside in our box near the big road. They were loud, and our car always swayed with the gusts of wind caused by them. Every time one drove by, I would try to make myself smaller to hide. I pressed my body so close to the side of the box that it hurt. This was not very brave of me. I felt bad inside. I hoped my friend did not see my fear.

The car stopped in front of a big house. The house was different from anyplace we had been to so far. We had been in a box, the Vet's office, the shelter, and now a house. We were greeted by several humans. They were all showing teeth and making funny high–pitched sounds as they grabbed us. The humans petted us and kissed us, and I felt warmth inside my body. We were not scared at all. Instead, we felt relieved and excited. We were relieved because we left the place called a *shelter*.

Although things were okay in the shelter, I noticed that some dogs were taken for a walk by a sad human. Those dogs never came back. Each time the sad human did this, they seemed to grow sadder. I overheard one of the humans saying it was a shame that the little puppies would be put to sleep soon. There was no room. I knew what that meant. The sad human would come for us soon. I cringed every time I heard the metal gate open. Was this it? Was this the time for us to be put to sleep?

On the last day, the metal gate opened, but it was not the sad human. A cheerful human took us all together and said, "Today is your lucky day!" That was when we were loaded into the back of the car to arrive at the house. I was relieved and happy, as were the others; I felt sad for the ones that were not lucky. *Why should luck determine if we live or die?*

The human girl at this big house had another dog already. She called him Bear. He would run up to her whenever she called his name. Then she would pet him and give him kisses. Bear. I liked Bear. He looked like me, only bigger. We both had black fur with brown on our legs. My littermates did not. They were all white or beige or a combination of both. I stood out from them because of my size and being the darkest in the group. My best friend was all white. She was small too, but still bigger than me. I liked that I resembled Bear. He was big and strong and had wise eyes. I hoped to grow up to be just like him. Bear sent me messages, too, just like Mom did. He told me to ask him anything. I bet Bear would have all the answers!

There was a family of humans that lived at this house. They all took care of different tasks related to us. The human girl that called after Bear was the primary caregiver, however. After the humans finished playing with us, they showed us our beds. We were still young, so they had to feed us with a fake teat and fake milk. Bear watched us closely; I watched him closely too. I thought about all the things I could learn from him. If I were to grow big, I would have to learn a lot.

Bear liked to go outside. There was a lot of grass there, and he would run and play. Sometimes Bear would go in the bushes and hide and then jump out. It was funny to watch. This place was so different from where Mom lived. I wished Mom could have felt the grass and run free. At that moment, I decided I would run for her. I would live my best life for Mom. I owed her that.

6

ANIMAL-SPEAK

I dreamt when I slept. Sometimes I dreamt of Mom. I cried in my sleep and pretended to drink from her. My mouth moved in sucking motions, but nothing came. It made me sad, and I was reminded of how much I missed her. My littermates and I were almost a month old. These humans also said we were too young to be away from our mother. They seemed truly angry about the situation that brought us here. We should never have been left. We should never have been taken away from Mom. I wondered why we were too. I would have to ask Bear. He seemed to know a lot of things.

Other dreams I had were interesting. In my favorite dream, I was a big, grey wolf. I was wild and free, but I was also close to a human, a woman. She was *my* human. I had imprinted on her and she did on me too. I asked Bear to explain imprinting to me. He said it was when one being attached themselves to another being through their energy. It was an unbreakable bond. Nothing could separate their bond, not time, space, or even death. I did not really understand this very well, but Bear said I would in time.

In my dream, my human and I walked together in the woods so she could gather plants and herbs. While she did this, she sang softly. Sometimes her singing was out loud and other times it was quieter; her mouth did not move but I, Wolf, could hear the song. I liked those times.

While she gathered her plants and herbs, I stayed close. Always alert. It was my job to protect her. Humans were capable of many things that I was unable to do, but they lost something along the way. They did not seem to know how to sense danger or shifts in energy. That is where I came in. I stood near my human and positioned myself so that I could see and feel everything around me in almost a full circle. I also felt vibrations in the earth that came up through my paws and smelled shifts in energy through the air and wind. I was exceptionally good at my job and protected my human well.

My dream-human was a healer. She helped people with her concoctions. She was able to smell sickness on them and knew which herbs to give them. She also helped them get rid of the dark energy that lived in their souls, through energy work My human also used her hands to touch and rub their skin so they could move better and feel better. Sometimes my human rubbed me, and it felt particularly good after a long run. I loved my human.

When I woke up from the dreams of my life as Wolf, I felt a sense of urgency. I must find my human. She was out there somewhere and needed me. How could I find her? Would she recognize me? I would have to ask Bear this as well.

My littermates and I spent most of our time running around playing, eating, and sleeping. The golden human, whose name was Jordan, spent a lot of time with us too. She taught us how to behave properly and not relieve ourselves inside the house. She taught us how to come to her when she called and mostly how to play and be happy. Most of my littermates played amongst themselves. I spent a lot of time with my best friend. We enjoyed rolling on the grass and practiced jumping. I liked to jump.

I also followed Bear a lot. Wherever Bear went, I followed. He never got angry. He liked me. Bear showed me many things that Jordan could not because she was human. Bear taught me how to purposely move my ears in the direction of sound. He taught me how to decipher different smells to determine what was going on. Humans gave off a scent when they were angry, sad, hurt, or happy. It was important to know what humans were feeling before you approached them. I was eager to learn everything.

Bear began teaching me a special gift. He called it Animal-Speak. The name was funny because it was not speaking like humans do with words. Bear said that all creatures are born with the ability for Animal-Speak, but humans forgot how because they were too busy learning human words. Humans. No tail, no fur, no Animal-Speak!

Animal-Speak is a way to communicate without words. It is the connection and relaying of messages through energy and non-verbal methods. Sometimes the speaker can make sounds like moans, groans, yips, howls, purring, and lip smacking. It also uses your body to relay moods and messages. Animal-Speak uses touch, smell, taste, sight, and sound. Ears can move toward a sound without moving our heads. We can smell things far away and taste things in the air that humans cannot. My favorite part of Animal-Speak, and maybe the most important for communicating at a distance, is using pictures in your mind and sending them to others far away.

Animal-Speak takes a lot of practice with humans, but it is extremely easy with other animals. Bear said to talk to everything with pictures. As I strengthened my natural abilities of communication, it would become easier to do with humans. I was not sure if that was true, but I trusted Bear. I sent pictures to everything—rabbits, groundhogs, beavers, mice, possums, and even insects. Insects were annoying. They were much too busy talking with each other and working to send messages back to me. I even tried to send pictures to the great big trees. Trees seemed to have a lot to say and were filled with old knowledge.

Jordan thought I was just following Bear for company, but

we were practicing many things and he talked to me all the time. The humans could not hear us talking. They were amazed at how well I followed Bear's lead. If only they understood that Bear was telling me what to do, and I was simply obeying him. The most important thing Bear told me was that I was in training. He knew I was Wolf and other creatures, before I came here as me. He said to remember all the things I learned from my other lives before because I would need the information someday. This was exciting but also a bit scary. Bear always laughed a bit when I was scared. Not in a mean way, but in a way that let me know this fear was only temporary. Bear told me that I was a great warrior, and someday my skills would be needed. I would not feel scared. I would feel excited and ready. When that time came, Bear said I would realize my purpose.

I had not thought about that before. My purpose. What was my purpose? Why was I sent here again? Why was I taken away from Mom? What job was I supposed to do? Why did I look different from the others? Why was I smaller? Would I find my human? Would I fit in? Would I be loved? I had so many questions. I asked Bear these questions and more. Some things he answered for me right away. Other things, he said I had to be patient. Patience meant learning to wait. This would prove to be one of the hardest lessons for me to learn.

7

NAMING DAY

*T*oday was naming day. We had been here for a week. We learned where everything was quickly. Since we all felt safe, we were able to grow in our bodies and into our personalities. We each had our own unique personality. Humans could tell the difference between us by how we behaved as well as by our fur. I was easiest to pick out for both reasons. I looked different, and I had a big personality!

Jordan gave all the littermates a name. My best friend was named Angel because she was sweet and kind and shy. I thought that was perfect for her. I was last to be named. Jordan named me Little Bear! She said that since I followed Bear everywhere and we looked similar, it was fitting to call me Little Bear. The others laughed; they thought it was silly to be named after Bear. They said I was a baby, but it made me incredibly happy and proud. I held my head up high and looked at Bear. He was very pleased. Angel liked my name too. I jumped up and down and ran in circles. I was so happy!

Jordan practiced our names with us. We were told to come when she called our name. I got mine right every time she called out "Little Bear." It was a lot of fun at first. Sometimes I would hear someone call my name, and I did not respond. It wasn't that I did not know what to do. I just didn't feel like it. I would smell the air first to make sure it was not an emergency, and if everything was okay, I just stayed where I was doing whatever I was doing. Jordan knew I was not listening on purpose. She said I was being stubborn. Maybe. I just wanted to do something else.

I learned everything that I was taught there, and I wanted to learn more. I got bored easily. Bear said that I was very smart, and in my other lives I'd already mastered these human tricks. That explained why things came easily to me. It was why I got bored quickly. Bear warned me about being idle. He said the worst thing a dog like me could do was to be idle. A dog like me. What did that mean?

"You will understand soon enough, Little One," Bear said. "Just remember to keep your mind busy. Practice and train your body. You will need these skills one day."

Sometimes I wished Bear would just tell me in plain words. Why did I always have to guess what he meant and wait? Sigh. I was getting impatient. Then I remembered what Bear had told me about being patient. I decided to run around the yard to pass the time and release some frustration. I ran as fast as I could, pretending to be Wolf chasing an intruder. The others started running after me. They could not catch up to me. I kept running, and it felt amazing! I picked up more speed and heard everyone make sounds of amazement. This felt great! I was a champion. I tried to go a little faster when I suddenly found myself face first in the ground. I rolled over a few times and lay there to catch my breath. Jordan called my name. "Little Bear!" I lifted my head up and saw her running to me. I stood up and shook my entire body from head to tail. I was okay. Jordan picked me up and gave me kisses. She asked me if I was okay. I licked her chin.

"You are such a fast runner! The fastest of everyone!" Jordan said.

I held my head up high. I was proud of myself. I enjoyed running fast. I added that to my list of training activities. I drank some water and then lay down for a little rest.

8

MOVING DAY

My littermates and I were being sent up north. Jordan had water coming from her eyes but was also showing her teeth. Bear said the water was called tears, and humans cry with tears when they are happy or sad. He taught me how to tell the difference. I think Jordan was both happy and sad because she would miss us, but she was also hopeful that we would find our forever home. Bear agreed.

I went for a last walk with Bear. I did not want to leave him. I was sad and afraid. Bear told me to be brave. This move was one step closer to finding my purpose, and I must be strong and brave. When I told him that I would miss him and still needed him, he laughed and reminded me that we were able to speak anytime we wanted. All that was required was for me to think of him and send pictures.

We had been practicing this for a while now. He would hide in the bushes, and I would send him a message. Then, if he got it, he would answer. We did this all day; we started close and then made the distance between us farther and farther apart. What I realized was that for the messages to be sent and received properly, I could not think of anything else. I had to focus on who I wanted to receive the message and what I wanted to say.

An expert like Bear was able to do many things at once and was able to hear messages even if they were not meant for him. He used to say that it was a blessing and a curse. Sometimes, you do not want to hear the thoughts of others. I didn't want to hear the insects. They were annoying. Except for butterflies. I liked butterflies.

Bear and I play-wrestled and then we licked one another, and I leaned on him. Bear said he was proud of me. He told me to remember my instincts and to be careful. He told me to be a good boy. He said he loved me. Then Bear walked away. Bear's tail was down. As tough as he was, his tail told me different on that day. He was sad. That made me sad, and my tail went down too. I thought of Mom, and I whimpered. Bear turned his head to me and sent me a silent message.

"Be strong, Little One. Your mom is at peace now with the ancestors. She is always with you. Do not be afraid. You have a big purpose ahead! I, too, will be with you forever." Then Bear disappeared into the house.

Oh, no! I had a feeling something had changed with Mom, but I was too busy learning and playing to really pay attention. Mom was gone from this earth. There would never be another chance to meet her face to face. My heart felt heavy. There was a lot of sadness and change to deal with today.

Jordan picked us all up, kissed us on the forehead, and put us in a box. I stayed close to Angel. Jordan said we had a long journey ahead. She touched all of us again, then picked me up one last time. She gave me kisses and pulled me close to her chest before putting me back with the others. Angel and I felt tired. We curled up together and fell asleep.

I do not know how much time passed. We were driving for an awfully long time with a nice woman who talked to us while she drove. She was also on the phone a lot, talking about us. We were called "rescues," and she was trying to find our forever home. I did not mind driving, but I still disliked the trucks. Angel was afraid. I curled up next to her and she seemed to feel better. I fell asleep again and dreamt of my days as Wolf.

In this dream, I saw my human. She was calling out to me. Her clothes were different from in my other dreams. Her clothes looked like what Jordan wore, whereas before she had on a beige animal pelt with a lot of beads. Her hair was long in both dreams but was worn differently. She was not collecting herbs. She was not in the woods. Everything was different, but I knew that it was her. I could smell her. I could sense that it was her. I turned my head in all directions, and then started running toward her. I hoped I would find my human soon. I woke up from the dream when a huge truck passed us on the road and shook the car hard.

I lifted my head on occasion to see what was going on. I changed my position so that I could keep my eyes on the lady driving and the outside. Angel shifted position too. She always kept her head on top of me. When I moved my head, Angel would move her head too. The window in the car was open. I twitched my nose quickly so that I could smell everything at once. We were moving fast and moving away from Jordan. I could smell a difference in the air. The trees were different. They had a different smell and different stories to tell. I wondered how far north we would go. Was there an end, or did the road just keep going farther and farther north? The birds above were flying in a pattern that looked like a letter V. They were good at keeping their lines straight. The leader showed them the way; after a while, the leader would fall back and another one would take that spot. The first leader would slow down until it was in the back. It seemed that the birds did this so as not to get too tired being the fastest and the first. Birds were smart.

We stopped a few times to get out and relieve ourselves. We were able to stretch. It felt good. Then we were put back in the box and the car started up again. Angel had a lot of questions. She wanted to know where we were going, would we live together forever, were we going to live with other animals or only humans? I did not have any answers for her. I hoped I would live with Angel. She was my best friend. We had been together since the very beginning. My stomach tightened with the thought of not being with Angel. I closed my eyes hoping I would stop thinking about this.

Somewhere in the distance I heard my human calling out. She was tired and scared. She just wanted peace and comfort.

"I'm coming, Human. I'm on my way!" I said.

I did not know if she heard me.

9

GO NORTH, YOUNG MAN

he car stopped and the engine turned off. We had arrived. I learned that the driver's name was Dawn. She had many dogs and cats that were not hers. She rescued them, cleaned them up, gave them medical attention, and then found them homes. Her cloak was also golden with purple running through it. I liked her.

Dawn brought us inside and gave us food and pretend–mom milk. She was on the phone a lot. It was a lot of work to run a Rescue. Dawn made appointments for us at the Vet. We would be checked out thoroughly by the doctors and given shots to keep us healthy. The others were seen first. They squirmed and yelped because the shots hurt.

"I am not going to yelp. I cannot let anyone see me weak. I am a warrior!" I told myself. Angel just looked at me. The doctor came over, and I stood as still as I could. I was rigid, like a tree. "Ouch!" I yelped. I looked around to see if anyone noticed. They heard me and made sad but loving sounds. Sigh. Maybe next time I wouldn't yelp. Bear popped in. He reassured me that it was okay. The shots hurt, but as I got older it would not hurt as much. I was happy to hear from Bear. I sent him back a message too. It was more like a million questions.

Bear said, "Just be patient, it will be what it is meant to be."

So, I took a deep breath and watched the others. Angel got her shot and she whimpered. When the humans put her back with us, she ran right over to me and I licked her wound. She calmed down. I loved Angel.

We were back in the crate and car. We were driving farther north. I knew this because Dawn said so, but also because the air smelled different. There were even more trees and plants that were unfamiliar to me. The roads were filled with more trucks and cars driving right on top of each other almost. The air smelled like chaos. Too many sounds crowded out nature's song. It was so loud. My head hurt. I tried to block out the noise and focus on nature. I wished I could hear those annoying insects now. I preferred their chatter to this noise. I hoped our forever home was not in a truck or filled with this noise. I heard Bear laughing.

"No, Little One, it will be in a good place. You'll see." Bear. I wished he was here with me now. I wished I was back home with Bear.

I heard Dawn talking and she said we were only five weeks old. Could that be? I felt like I had been in this body for a very long time. Was I only five weeks old? I lay down in the crate to think about this, and my mouth did the sucking motion. I wanted my mom. I drifted off to sleep with Angel's paw in my face.

We stayed with Dawn for some time. We ate and played and listened to her talking. Dogs and other types of animals came and went from her house, as they found permanent homes.

Wolf was running north. He ran fast and passed the trees leaving a trail of wind behind him. As he ran, he was listening intently for signals. There was no danger. He was running toward his human. I felt Wolf inside me. My legs twitched while I slept. I was running. Wolf and I were one and the same.

"I'm coming, Human! I'm coming!"

ADOPTION DAY

*D*awn drove us again to a new place. She carried us inside a big house. She set up a table with paperwork and all our medical records and history. There were a lot of other dogs and puppies there. The humans greeted us and wished us luck. They hoped other humans would come by to see all of us and bring us home. Adoption was the word everyone used. From what I gathered, adoption meant we would become part of a family and live with them forever. This was exciting. It also made me nervous. What if the wrong human picked me? What if I was not picked at all? Would Angel stay with me forever? I turned to look at her. She was a little nervous. She came over to me and leaned on me. I almost fell over because she was leaning on me so hard.

"Don't worry, Angel. It will be okay," I told her.

I hoped I was right.

We were put outside on the grass inside a circular fence. We were happy to be on the grass. The others were running in circles and playing. Angel and I stayed close to the fence, watching the others. I wished I could just have fun and not think so much. It seemed to me that thinking sometimes stopped you from living.

Hm. I would have to think about that some more when I settled in for the night; meanwhile, I continued to watch and observe. I looked around and saw many humans walking around. They were showing their teeth and made high–pitched sounds at all the dogs. I did not see my human. I tried hiding behind the others. Angel was close by me.

She whispered to me, "Will we be together forever?"

I did not know. I did not think so. I was scared again.

I called out to Bear. "Why must we be separated? Why can't we stay together?" I asked him.

Bear calmly replied, "It is the way of the humans. Don't worry. It will be what is meant be."

Then Bear quickly added, "Remember if you use Animal-Speak, you will always be connected to Angel. Just like you and I are forever connected. No one can take that from you."

Bear was right. I took a deep breath and waited.

I sat down with Angel next to me. Angel and I talked to each other. I let her know that a good human would bring her home and that she would be happy and loved. I told her what Bear said about Animal-Speak. She kissed me. I nuzzled her neck. We stayed this way for a while. The others were being lifted out of the fence and we yelped goodbye to them. They looked back at us and wagged their tails. They seemed happy.

I smelled the air. I smelled it again. Something was being carried in the air. Not something, *someone*! I smelled my human nearby. I stood up to get a closer look. Another human came over to the fenced area and looked directly at me. I turned to Angel and told her I loved her. I told her she had her own purpose to fulfill. We looked at each other and then I was lifted out of the fence. I heard Angel whimper, and then a few moments later she made happy sounds. I peeked over to her and saw that she was licking the face of a new human. Angel found her family. She would be okay. This made me happy.

I saw a human with two smaller humans. My heart began to

beat faster. *My human*. I saw a flash of Wolf in my mind. He was excited and happy. Yes! My human arrived. I was carried over to them, held by my front armpits with my body dangling. This was not the most majestic of positions. I was a little embarrassed. I hoped I did not relieve myself in this position. The smaller humans, one male and one female, were making little love sounds; the big human, *my* human, took a deep breath. She took me from the human who was carrying me. I smelled her skin. I remembered her smell. My heart beat faster. My human smelled like home! I curled up on her arm and rested my head on her wrist. I could feel her pulse. I closed my eyes. I was exhausted yet relieved to find her. I fell asleep, but not completely. I still heard my human's voice. She was speaking to her children.

She said, "Well, that's it then. I guess we are adopting him."

The boy and girl squealed and laughed. They were so excited. I found my human! Or my human found me. Either way, we were together again. Did she remember me? Did she remember Wolf? There was so much to learn and teach, but for right now, I decided to just enjoy the moment.

There was nothing nicer than being in my human's arms. The small humans were rubbing me, and there was a lot of talking between them. We walked to a car, and there was a box with a blanket inside of it. My human gently placed me in the box and gave instructions to the girl to make sure the box stayed steady. The girl showed her teeth to me and the boy.

"I knew it!" she said.

My human just grunted, "Hm," but then smiled.

It was not a long ride at all. We passed many houses and trees. The sun was shining, and it felt warm on my fur. I sat up in the box the entire time. I looked around at everything. I crouched down when a truck passed, and the girl let out a sound. "Aww," she said. She knew that I did not like trucks.

We stopped in front of a house and then turned into a

narrow road next to it. This seemed like a good house. It smelled nice, a mixture of flowers, trees, and good food. I twitched my nose quickly so I could get my bearings. Bear taught me that. He told me to always get your bearings right away, so that you would always be able to find your way back home. The street in front of the house was quiet. The street to the side was a little busier. I could smell other animals. Not just dogs, but tree climbers, ground animals, and other four-legged creatures I would soon learn about. The house had a lot of stairs to climb. I had to be carried upstairs. I was still too small to take the stairs myself.

I paid attention to the relationship between my human and the small humans. Every group has an order: a leader, workers, and security. A good group works together to get everything accomplished and to keep the group safe. The little humans called my human Mommy; she was the pack leader. The boy and girl were her children. The boy was older but not by much. They followed Mommy's lead. They were almost equal with each other, but the boy was still in charge of the girl. I would have to find my position in the pack. This could take some time. I would need to get older. I was only six weeks old, after all.

Mommy decided to keep my name, Little Bear, because I already answered to it. I was happy they kept my name, and I told Bear about it right away. He was very pleased. They practiced calling me and I came running every time I heard my name. Mommy took me around the apartment. She carried me upstairs, and I could smell this was where the little humans slept. Back downstairs, Mommy showed me where she slept. This was a nice room.

We also had an outside area. The ground was wood, and there were wooden bars around it. Above was a big tree that hung over to give shade from the sun. Mommy had pots with plants and herbs. I smelled everything I could reach. I was still very small. I sent Bear images of my new home. He was happy for me.

Mommy picked me up and said, "Welcome home, Little One! You are safe now. No one will hurt you."

Little One—that is what Bear called me! I liked this place. I felt safe. I felt loved. I was *home*.

TRAINING

There was much to learn here. I had to learn the rules of the house, which included areas that were not for me, things I could not bite (which was everything except for some toys), where things were, what I could and could not play with, how to relieve myself outside and never inside, where my food and water bowls were so I could eat and drink, and where I was allowed to sleep.

Mommy was told that I must be kept in the crate. She brought home a crate on the day of my adoption. We also had gone to a store that was for animal supplies only. There were so many things there. Mommy carried me around because I had not gotten all my shots from the Vet yet. She did not want me to pick up any germs from other dogs. Mommy, the boy, and the girl picked up many different things for me, including a leash. I quickly remembered my mom on a leash holding her back from reaching us when we were taken away. Even inside her kennel, Mom was not allowed off her leash, always restricted, never free. I did not think that would happen to me. I hoped not. Aside from the leash, there were the two bowls for food and drink, some toys, and some treats. I never had a toy all my own. They also bought a round soft cushion that Mommy said was a bed for me. I felt very special. All these things for me!

Mommy set up the crate in the main room. From inside, I could see the couch where they sat and talked and watched TV. I could tell by her energy that she was not happy about something. She looked at the crate and her mouth made a weird shape. It made her whole face look sad. She placed a soft towel inside as well as one of my new toys. She stared at it for a few minutes, thinking. I could tell she was torn between following directions and not liking the crate very much.

My very first night at home, Mommy placed me inside the crate. I went in and lay down. It was comfortable. I could see through the bars, and I liked the blanket and snuggly toy she had placed inside. I was quiet. The children went upstairs. I could see through the apartment windows that it was dark outside. Then, it was dark inside. I heard Mommy lie down in her bedroom next door. I started crying. Loudly. I wanted Mommy! I had never slept alone in all my days. I panicked. I wanted Angel and my other littermates. I wanted Mom. I wanted Bear! I felt alone and scared. *Mommy! Mommy! Mommy!*

I heard Mommy get up and walk toward me. I kept crying till I saw her face. Then I cried softly and stuck my paw outside the crate bars.

Mommy started to talk to me.

"I'm sorry, Baby. You must stay in your crate. They said it's important for your training to sleep in there."

I heard it in her voice that she was sad. She was also confused and torn, because she wanted to take me out and hold me close but was trying to follow the directions of the experts. I continued to cry but softer. Mommy lay down on the couch next to the crate and held my paw.

Bear told me, "Calm down. It is only for a little while. Do what is asked, and you will get more."

I did not know what that meant, but I trusted Bear. He always taught me well. I lay down and closed my eyes, with my paw in Mommy's hand. Mommy fell asleep on the couch. I slept a little but woke up often. I heard noises, and I looked at Mommy to make sure she was okay.

When Mommy woke up, she said hello to me right away. She let me out of the crate and carried me outside. I was still too small for stairs. I put that on my list of things to learn. It felt so good to relieve myself. She let me run around for a little bit before she carried me upstairs to the apartment. Mommy reminded me where my food and water were kept and said my name often. She also called me "Baby." I wondered if Mommy was starting to remember me, to remember Wolf.

I looked into her eyes when she held me. She looked into my eyes. Something weird happened at that moment. It was as if we became one and understood each other completely. I felt her presence from today and from the past. Now I understood *imprinting*. We imprinted on each other. She kissed my face, and I licked hers. I loved Mommy. I would do anything for Mommy. I would protect Mommy. . . as soon as I got bigger.

The children came downstairs and went to me right away. We were playing and snuggling. It felt like when I was with the others and Angel. Mommy said the little humans were my skin-siblings, my brother and sister. The children laughed. She also said I was her fur-baby. The children laughed again. It took me a while to understand that, but when I finally did, I laughed inside too!

That night, Mommy proceeded to put me inside the crate again. She said "Good night. I love you," and walked into her room. I started crying again. I did not want to sleep alone. How could I protect Mommy from inside this cage? *Mommy! Mommy! MOMMY!*

Mommy came back inside. She knelt in front of the cage.

"Baby. You must stay in the crate so you do not have accidents in the house. I'm sorry, sweetheart."

I saw her pictures. I understood what she said. Mommy talked in pictures! The pictures were inside her head as she spoke words out loud. She knew Animal-Speak! I was so excited to learn this. I asked Mommy if she would keep me company. I sent her pictures from my mind. Mommy sighed.

"Okay, Little One. I'll keep you company for a little while, but *not* the whole night." She lay down and held my paw. I started talking to Bear and told him what I discovered. He said that Mommy was a special human but may not realize that she knew Animal-Speak. He warned me to be patient. I fell asleep while talking to Bear. When I opened my eyes, Mommy was not there. It was not dark anymore. I cried out to her. *Mommy!* She came in right away.

"Good morning, Baby! Did you sleep well? Let's go do pee-pee."

I was so excited to see her. I wagged my tail and stood up in the crate. Mommy laughed. I liked when Mommy laughed. It sounded like a song.

The next night was the same. Mommy put me in the crate. She said, "Good night. I love you," and walked into her room. I started crying again. *Mommy! Mommy! Mommy!* Mommy came back inside. She looked at me, right in my eyes. I instantly sent her a message.

"I won't have an accident! I won't."

Mommy made a little grunting sound and then opened the crate. She picked me up and held me to her face. "NO accidents, Little One!" I kissed her face and she laughed. She carried me inside her room and put me on the floor. It was soft and fluffy. Mommy climbed up on the bed and said goodnight. No! I wanted to sleep *with* her on the bed. Mommy told me to be quiet and go to sleep or she would put me back in the crate. I decided to be quiet and lay down under the window next to her bed. I could see the door, the window, and Mommy from this position. "It's all about positioning," I heard in my head. Ahhh, yes. I remembered.

I was a good boy for most of the night. I walked around the room, the living room, the kitchen, and drank a little water. Not too much. I did not want an accident. Then I went back to Mommy's room and took my place under the window. I could see her sleeping. I could hear her dreams. She was sad. She was scared. Poor Mommy. I began to cry out, softly. I stood on my back legs but could not reach the top of the bed. *Mommy!*

She opened her eyes and said "Oh, Baby. You okay?"

With one hand hanging over the side of the bed, she lifted me up and placed me next to her. I could feel her heartbeat. It reminded me of Mom. I curled up and listened to her heartbeat while Mommy rubbed my back. Mommy's heartbeat slowed down a little, and her breathing got softer. Mine did too. I heard Mommy whisper, "I love you" before she drifted off. I read her messages before falling asleep. Mommy was not sad. She was no longer scared. She was at peace. There was love. We fell asleep together. It was the best sleep ever.

I did not want to have an accident, but I had to relieve myself. Mommy was still sleeping. The children had not come downstairs yet. I stood on Mommy and tried to yell. It was a funny sound. I tried again. Mommy opened her eyes and showed her teeth.

"Baby! You found your bark!"

She scooped me up and took me outside right away. AHHHHHHHH. That felt good. I told Bear about finding my bark. He was proud.

Mommy was the leader of our pack, as I mentioned earlier. She oversaw all of us. All rules were made by her. The children tried to tell me what to do. Sometimes I would listen, but mainly I did not. They were my equals. They were bigger and older, but that did not mean they could tell me what to do. Sometimes I used my teeth to nip them, to challenge them. Mommy didn't like that at all. I was put in the crate when I used my teeth. Mommy was mad; she worried about the children and me. Poor Mommy. She carried a lot of worry in her mind. I must be a good baby so I could help her.

Sister sometimes used her teeth on my ears. Not hard, but

gentle nips. She never got put in the crate for using her teeth. I wondered why there were different rules.

There were rules called chores. Chores were little jobs to keep things clean and neat. Mommy would yell at Brother and Sister to help with the chores. I always hid under the couch or bed when Mommy yelled. This made the children laugh. "You are scaring Little Bear," Sister would say. Mommy would sigh and stop yelling. I would creep out and sit by her until she lifted me up so I could lick her face. I felt proud. I handled the situation, and no one stayed mad at each other. I was a clever dog. I did not know if they realized I was the reason for maintaining the peace.

I remembered life as Wolf one day when I was napping. Wolf was walking in circles around the camp. My human and two others were in camp, cooking and packing things in a bag made from animal skin. The older human was a man. They called him Brother. The second oldest was almost the same age as my human and the smallest was a few years younger. They were girls. It was during this memory that I realized that my new brother, sister, and Mommy were Wolf's humans, except they were siblings back then!

Wolf's man-human was packing some things for a trip. He was going to battle. He was leaving the two girl-humans alone at camp. He walked over to Wolf and petted him and hugged him around the neck.

"Look out for them, Wolf. You must protect them while I am away," he said.

Wolf nudged the man-human with his head and trotted over to the girl-humans. The older one had tears running down her face. Wolf reached up with his tongue and licked the tears away. The younger girl grabbed the older one's hand. With her free hand, she reached out and petted Wolf. Wolf stood close to them. He would protect them always.

LEARNING THE ROPES

I was getting bigger. I could jump up on the bed without help, and I hardly ever stayed in the crate. Mommy did not like the crate. When I was inside it, she felt as if *she* was inside the crate, and it made her feel anxious. I tried awfully hard to behave. Sometimes, I could not help being bad. Humans had a lot of rules that are not natural to dogs.

For example, my skin-siblings had some friends over. I nipped at one of the friends. My job was to protect my family, and I needed to make sure these friends knew that. It was just a little nip. A warning. My humans didn't understand that. Most humans do not. They do not have good instincts and don't understand the subtle cues that animals use to express themselves.

I talked to Bear about this. He said that humans do not like dogs that bite or nip. I should find another way to express myself and to protect them. Mommy didn't really get angry with me. She understood on some level, but she could not let me nip at people either. The children did not understand though; they thought I was being bad. Because of this incident, they put me inside the bedroom with the door closed. I was not allowed to be with them. This made me sad and angry. I wanted to be with them. I wanted to protect my family!

At first, I would bark and bark. After a while, I just lay down and listened. I heard them laughing or talking. That was okay. There was nothing to be worried about. I imagined myself breaking down the door in case I heard any sounds I did not like. If anyone hurt my family, I would find a way to get out of this room and rip them apart! I imagined being Wolf protecting my humans against other wild creatures. Wolf was extremely strong and fierce. There were many times when he had to put his life on the line to protect his humans. He was a warrior and great defender. I was sure, if I had to, I would be able to do the same.

Meanwhile, I just lay in the room and listened. My head popped up when I heard the friends walking down the hall or stairs. They were leaving. I would be able to come out now. When the door opened, I bolted out and raced toward our front door. I barked loudly and stomped my front feet, landing with thumps. Sister laughed and said I was behaving like a punk. Whatever. I am Wolf! This is *my* territory. Sister picked me up and gave me kisses. My heart was beating fast, and my breath was deep and heavy. She petted me, and I calmed down. I liked to be held by Sister.

Sometimes, one of Mommy's friends would come over. Mommy never liked to put me in the other room. I appreciated this. She taught me to "Stop," "Behave," and "Give kisses only." I learned these things quickly so that I would not be put inside behind the closed door.

Mommy would sit on the couch with her friend. I did not mind this friend, not exactly. I *did* need to make sure he knew I was in charge. I would jump up on the couch and sit either on Mommy's lap or right in between them. When I did this, Mommy laughed a little. She understood. I sat with my back toward Mommy, facing the friend. I did not bark. There was no point in that. I just stared.

My message was this: "You can stay because Mommy said you could, but never forget I am here. I will bite you if need be." The friend did not like this behavior too much. He would try to get me down or chase me into the room. Mommy would get angry with him and defend me. That's right, friend! It's me and Mommy forever!

Once I found my voice, I liked to use it. I liked to bark. When I saw people outside the window, I barked. Sometimes it was simply to say hello, and other times it was because I did not know who they were, and I was warning them to stay away. Occasionally, I barked because I didn't like them. I could tell by their smell that something was "off" with them. Smells carried quite a distance. It is something that is subtle to humans, but I could distinguish good or bad by the smell of them.

I also would bark at squirrels. There was something unsettling about squirrels. They moved around so quickly, chattering nonsense, teasing me from outside, leaping from branch to branch to ground. There was one particular squirrel that would come onto our deck and take Mommy's tomatoes that she was waiting to pick. Squirrel was fat and greedy. He did not need to eat them. He did it because he was selfish. He would take a tomato and eat only half of it, then leave the other half on the railing. He made quite a mess. Mommy got annoyed because she wanted the tomatoes for a salad.

I barked at Squirrel a lot. He was smart, though. He knew I could not catch him. He would also sit on the lowest branch just above the railing and make these chattering sounds at me. He was laughing at me. One time, he even came right onto the screen of the outside door and just hung there. I leapt at the door with all my force. He scurried away but stayed close enough to be annoying. It was very frustrating. I did not like squirrels, and I especially did not like *this* Squirrel.

Mommy decided to teach me to bark quieter, or "talk." She used hand gestures and repeated words to me so I would make the connection. I also received treats when I did as she asked.

One day when I was barking excessively, she said, "No barking, just talk," moving her hand from high to low. I stopped barking and began to use a series of throat noises, whines, and whimpers all together in a long string pretending I was a human talking. Mommy was very proud of me for listening.

When humans talk, they move their mouth and use sounds from their throat. They can go on and on for a while forming words. The tone changes slightly depending on if they are happy, angry, or sad. After I put my string of sounds together, along with standing straight and stamping my paws, Mommy showed her teeth and laughed. She said I was very smart. I got a treat, head rubs, and kisses too!

Sometimes, very rarely, I howled. The sound came from deep inside. It began as a low rumble then built up until it released from my throat. It was the most satisfying thing I have ever felt. I was like Wolf, throwing my head up and releasing a slow, long howl. I pursed my lips together to form a circle and let the howl travel far away. Howls made me feel primal and connected to the earth. It was an ancient way of communicating that I instinctively knew.

The times when I howled, I was answering the sounds from a firetruck or alarm. It was a way to acknowledge an emergency and report it to other beings. Mommy and Sister loved hearing my howl. They always came running inside to watch me and laughed in excitement. They told me I was like a little wolf. Did they finally remember I *was* Wolf? I believed Mommy was starting to remember. I would stop howling when they came to me. They had received the warning and responded; no need to exaggerate. Howling was not something to be taken lightly.

Brother was a little different. He liked to be alone and disliked my fur getting on his things. I was not allowed in his room because of my fur. He loved me but didn't really show it in the same ways that Mommy and Sister did. I understood, though. He was male. Males have different ways and different responsibilities.

I liked to watch Brother. He was very smart. Sometimes, I felt he was frustrated. He was trying to find his purpose; he had an idea of what he needed to do but was still young in human years. He was a good protector. He knew how to move quietly like a lion, slow and steady and silent. He also watched everyone and everything. He didn't speak much, but I could hear his thoughts and knew he was always thinking. He had good instincts. I remembered him from my days as Wolf. He was the same then, too. I wished Brother could use Animal-Speak; I could talk to him about this and maybe help him feel less frustrated. I, too, was trying to find my purpose. I knew part of it was to find Mommy, but what was I supposed to do now that I found her?

PREPARATIONS

*H*umans are funny creatures. They leave the house for hours and come back tired and cranky. The days that they do not leave for hours, they are cleaning and going in and out bringing home food and other things, and again are tired and cranky. I do not think humans understand what life is about; rather, they think of life as a series of chores and acquisitions, instead of enjoying life and being present in each moment. The feel of the Sun shining on your back, watching a butterfly flutter about, rolling around in the grass, listening to the songs of the wind, or sitting next to each other and listening to each other's heartbeats; these are the things that matter most. Humans do not understand we are pack animals. We rely on each other to survive. Without our pack, we are lost, confused, and afraid. Sometimes, most times, we are even sad.

My humans were not home all the time. Work and chores kept them busy for most of the day. Mommy made sure to take care of me before she left the house; she always took great care of me. We would go for a nice morning walk, come home for breakfast, and sometimes she would toss my toy for me to play fetch with her for a few minutes. We always had time for some snuggles, even on the days that she was rushing. When Mommy was ready to leave, she always gave me a kiss and said "Goodbye, Baby. I will be back. Be a good boy. I love you!" Every morning was the same; I knew this meant I would be alone for a long time.

I was so happy when my family came home. It did not matter the length of time they were gone; I was just so happy to see them. While it was lonely at home without them, I kept busy. I walked around the apartment, I practiced the stairs, jumped on things, I practiced my listening skills, drank a little water, and slept a lot.

I made sure I did not neglect my security duties by over-sleeping. Walking around the apartment was not solely for exercise, but it was surveillance. I needed to use all my senses to ensure that there was no threat to the home.

Brother and Sister usually came home before Mommy. Sometimes I would come out, and sometimes I would not. I always greeted them if they were with friends; but if they came home alone, I sometimes remained under the bed or couch and just listened. One thing Bear taught me was the importance of being invisible while listening intently for clues. Obviously, I was not able to be invisible; our physical bodies remain. However, I learned how to hide and walk quietly so that no one could hear me. I learned that from watching Brother. The only thing that gave me away were the pendants that hung from my necklace. If I moved very slowly, they would not clink. Then I could peek my head around the corner and watch what Brother or Sister were doing. A few times, they turned around and were startled by my presence. Sister would laugh and say, "What a creep!" I knew she meant it lovingly.

When Mommy came home, I always ran out to greet her. The joy I felt seeing her again was like nothing I could describe. I would try and show my teeth like she did and wagged my tail hard. She was just as happy to see me too. Mommy always seemed heavier and darker when she came home as compared to when she left in the morning. There was so much stress and negativity attached to her at the end of the workday. I would let Mommy pet me, and I kissed her and acted silly. This seemed to help that heavy darkness leave Mommy. Another help was our walks. We would always go for a nice walk after her day away.

One day, we were walking on our long walk and I came across a branch. I picked it up. I could barely keep it in my mouth, but I managed by clenching my back teeth tightly. The branch was very long, too. It took up the whole path; no one was able to pass me. Mommy let me carry it. I carried this branch for most of our walk, stopping occasionally to move saliva around my mouth and readjust my grip. The neighborhood humans that saw me laughed and squealed. Mommy was very proud of me.

"Such a strong little one. And so smart!" she said.

I did not know why it was so important to me to carry this big branch. I just wanted to, and it seemed as if it was the right thing to do. I decided to drop the branch a few blocks from home. I moved it along the ground and covered it with some leaves. I kicked a lot of leaves on it with my back legs but also used my nose to move the leaves around to a specific area.

I used this nose trick when I wanted to hide things. One day, a stranger on the street gave me a treat because she said I was such a good boy. I carried it for a little while then decided to hide it for another time. I was not in the mood to eat it right away. I used my front paws to dig a little hole, dropped the treat inside, and then used my nose to cover it with leaves. I took a step back to look at my work. I was very pleased. It was well hidden. Once satisfied, we continued our walk.

Mommy really enjoyed our walks. Sometimes, she complained and was annoyed at the beginning. Brother and Sister were supposed to walk me when they got home. I knew she was tired, but I liked walks with Mommy the best. She would talk to me, let me smell things and explore. I would jump up on the high bricks which made me the same height as

Mommy. Jumping onto the wall always impressed Mommy and everyone who saw me. All my practicing at home was paying off!

There were many other four–legged creatures in the neighborhood; a lot of dogs and cats, but also others that we saw at a distance. Mommy loved to see them. I never barked at them because they made Mommy happy. Also, I could tell they were very gentle creatures. Mommy called them deer. The deer were sweet and timid. They liked to stay together in groups made up of mothers and their young. There were no adult male deer in these groups. The males usually only came around once a year and they carried big antlers on top of their heads. It was something to see, and I wondered if the antlers were heavy on their heads.

The female deer seemed confused and anxious. What was once a beautiful forest was now filled with homes and gardens belonging to humans. There were not many safe areas for the deer to take care of their young. There were also unnatural threats that were outside their understanding. Cars. Cars raced quickly up the road and sometimes deer were hit when trying to cross the street. Losing a member of their herd affected them; they were saddened. A baby deer that becomes orphaned must be adopted by another mother in the group to survive. Knowledge is transferred to the young by instinct and by example. With every change in terrain, their old knowledge does not apply. The mothers must learn to navigate new areas while teaching their young these new lessons; the lessons taught to the young suffer because things are ever changing and uncertain.

I was only allowed to walk outside with a harness and a leash, which Mommy or one of the kids held. This was primarily due to the fear of me running wild and getting hit by a car. Mommy also was concerned that I would run from her and get lost. I was an excellent runner, faster than any other dog in the neighborhood; I did not know this for a fact, but I could sense it. My legs were strong, and I was the perfect weight. I loved running fast. Mommy could not keep up with me when she tried to run with me attached to the leash. At least she tried. I missed the days of running free with Bear. I wished I could run free here; but we did not have a yard, and the streets were filled with cars.

I remembered days as Wolf running through the woods at top speed, dodging trees, jumping logs, and feeling the wind hit my face. So many days running free as Wolf. I chased deer back then, smaller creatures too. I was praised for my captures in those days.

One day while we were walking, Mommy squealed. It was not the happy sound I heard when she showed teeth. This was a different sound; it was laced with disgust and disappointment. I had been digging on our walk and found an underground burrow of little creatures. I grabbed one and secured it in my mouth. I proudly walked home expecting praise for my capture, like in the days of Wolf. Mommy had not noticed it was dangling out of my mouth for several blocks, until she glanced down at me and saw the tail swinging back and forth on one side of my mouth. That was when she squealed.

"Oh, no! Little Bear! Drop it," she said. I did not listen. This was my capture! We stood there for a while with Mommy telling me to let it go or drop it. I refused. Mommy said I was being stubborn. Yes. I was.

There was a part of Mommy that was impressed with me, but a greater part that wanted me to drop it. She was confused. She knew this was natural behavior for me but also did not like any creatures to be harmed. Mommy did not allow me to bring my prize home. She walked me to the back of the house and told me to leave it outside near the bushes. I understood that I would not be allowed to bring it inside. Sigh. I dropped the little creature under the bush. I didn't even bother to cover it with leaves. What was the point? I was not allowed in this area usually. I would never be able to get to it again. We started walking up the back stairs. I stopped and looked down in the direction of my capture. I looked at it for a while. It was not easy to find underground dens and move quickly enough to capture one of the creatures on the first try. It was a great capture. Swift, silent, and precise! I told Bear about it. At least *he* was proud.

We walked up the stairs and went inside. I did not get a treat right away. Mommy was not happy with me; I had not listened to her. She did not praise me for my capture. She told Brother and Sister, and they made weird faces and sounds. Humans!

I lay down on my cushion and rested my head on my front paws. I looked at them sadly. Humans are pathetic. They don't understand anything. Poor, pathetic humans! I stared at Mommy with my eyes big and full of disappointment.

"I feel you staring at me, Baby," she said.

Good! Feel my eyes burning into your soul! I was not happy with Mommy at that moment.

Mommy took a deep breath and walked over to me. She crouched down and petted my head.

"You are an incredibly good hunter, Little One! You did a great job. I just don't want little creatures hurt or killed and definitely not in the house."

She kissed the top of my head. I got a treat and she whispered, "Such a good boy and a great hunter!" Hm.

In that moment, all my bad feelings left me, and I felt proud of myself. I was a *great* hunter! Mommy was proud. I just must learn the human ways. I jumped off my cushion and started playing with some toys. I pretended they were creatures, and I was digging them up and capturing them. It was fun to play, and it made Mommy laugh. I saw her watching me out of the corner of my eyes. She especially liked when I would toss the toy in the air and then pounce on it. I growled at the toy and shook it fiercely with my head while gripping it in my mouth. When I was done, I walked around the apartment with the toy in my mouth, showing everyone my capture.

ADVENTURES

I got used to our car quickly. I would jump right in the back seat. Sometimes we would go for a long drive and go to a house where there were other humans from our clan. I could smell that they belonged to us. There was one human that Brother and Sister called Grandma. Grandma was an Elder. I never acted crazy around her. When I approached her, I did it very slowly and kissed her gently. I liked Grandma. She had a lot of love, but she kept it close to her. She was guarded. I could smell sadness and anxiety on her all the time. It was as if she was not certain of the path she chose; this uncertainty made her question all her choices. She did not trust her instincts. I remembered Mom told us the day we were taken from her to trust our instincts. Instincts should never be doubted. Humans tend to doubt their instincts and that made them sad and confused.

Grandma always showed her teeth when we visited. She loved to see us all. There were two other dogs and a few cats that lived there. The dogs were strange. They didn't use Animal-Speak. I tried to talk to them and got no response. This made me curious, so I would climb on them or smell them and lick their ears. They would get annoyed with me sometimes and try to move away from me. The cats were strange, too. They would not let me come near them. What a weird way to be.

There was plenty of room in this house. I liked to run around and smell things. The others seemed to find me funny because I had energy. I was younger than the other animals, but I think I had more energy because Mommy always made sure to keep me active. Grandma laughed when I would run and leap up on things. I was an incredible leaper! I would pretend I was jumping from one cliff to another in the woods. It was fun and exciting. In my mind the cliffs were separated by water. I would take a running start and leap off one and stretch my body as long as I could and then land on the other cliff. When I landed, I would always turn around to see who was watching. I liked when people watched my athletic abilities. Unless I missed my mark. Then, I would feel embarrassed and slowly walk in the other room and lay down. I would rest my head on my legs and replay the jump in my mind. *Where did I go wrong? What did I miscalculate?* I would do it right the next time!

One hot day at Grandma's house, Mommy put me inside this big fenced–in water thing. She held me, and I moved my legs. She wanted me to learn to swim. I didn't really like that. I felt nervous and the water smelled funny, not like a stream or fresh water. It did make me feel less hot though. I did not like swimming. In fact, I really don't like water too much. I preferred to dig and run in the forest. Mommy didn't keep me in for long. She knew I was not happy in this pool.

Other car adventures included going to the beach. Mommy would let me run free off the leash on the sand. I would run fast and far. Mommy would make a special sound with her mouth that sounded like a little bird's song. Whenever I heard that sound, I would stop and turn to look at her. She would motion with her hands hitting her legs and I would race back to her. I loved running free! The beach was lovely. There was salt in the air, and everything smelled fresh and clean. I stayed away from the water though. I got too close to it one time so that my toes got wet. I didn't like that feeling. I stayed far away from the shoreline after that.

Mommy would take me to a park so that I could smell new things. I liked adventures. I liked to walk and hike and meet other dogs. Some dogs were friendly, while others kept to themselves. I did make many friends at the park though. We would see each other and get excited and kiss each other and jump around. It reminded me of when I was little with Angel and the Others. It was nice to be around other dogs. I thought about Angel and wondered how she was doing. I hadn't been able to talk to her for a long time. Bear said that sometimes dogs become too domesticated and forget how to communicate at a distance. This reminded me of how special my life was with Mommy. She never tried to change me or stop me from doing things. She only stopped me if it would hurt me or the children, or if I did something gross or disruptive, like accidents in the house and chewing the wall. Sometimes, I thought that Mommy was becoming more dog–like and less human–like. Maybe I was helping her find her past human self? I wondered if Angel thought of me; I hoped she knew I thought of her often.

One day we went on a car adventure to a place that was even more crowded than where we lived. From the smell of things, it was south of home. Mommy called it a family vacation. The drive was long. When we stopped driving, we went into a building that had many separate rooms. We stayed in a room that had two beds, a bathroom, a small cold box for food, and a sink. The room smelled like many different humans; they were not present but were here before. After I relieved myself outside the room, we went inside, and I immediately started my surveillance. Mommy brought in the crate. I looked at the crate without moving my head. I did not want to even acknowledge it.

We slept in the beds all together. It was fun. I jumped from one bed to the other and made Brother, Sister, and Mommy laugh. The next morning, I had to stay in the crate all day while they went out. Mommy said she was sorry but that it was the hotel's rules. I hated being inside the crate.

Someone came in the room while they were gone. She was cleaning and moving things around. I barked and barked. *This is exactly why I should not be in a crate! How can I protect our things from inside here?* When my humans came back, they showed their teeth and let me out of the crate. I was happy to see them and happy to get out of the crate. I tried to tell Mommy about the strange person who came in the room; she did not seem to care. She seemed happy that the room was cleaned and in order.

Mommy let me sleep on the strange bed with her and Sister again. I lay down next to her feet and faced the door. I was ready in case I needed to protect anyone. When they fell asleep, I jumped down and surveyed the room. I smelled the air from under the door. I jumped onto the other bed, but Brother told me to get down. I forgot that he disliked fur. I went back to Mommy's bed and snuggled between Mommy and Sister. They never minded my fur. I took a deep breath and watched the door. I held my ears up; this was important for listening. I moved them in various directions to hear things from all angles. Even when I closed my eyes, my ears were working. Suddenly, someone walked close to the door of the room and stood in front of the door. I let out a low, deep growl. That was a warning. *Stay back! Stay away!* I did it again. After they walked away, I settled back down with ears up.

After a few days, we went back in the car. I could smell we were heading home. I enjoyed looking outside the window and seeing the trees go by. Mommy opened my window a little. I liked feeling the wind hit my face, and I kept my mouth open so that I could taste the different things as we drove through. Whenever a truck drove by, I crouched down low onto the seat. I still did not like trucks and probably never would.

Mommy looked at me and said, "It's okay, Baby. It won't hurt you."

Mommy understood me. She never made me feel bad for being afraid.

15

FORGIVENESS

I liked my life here, although it was not always easy. Sometimes, Mommy would get mad at all of us. When she yelled, I would hide under the bed. I stayed there until Mommy called me. She always hugged me and said she was sorry. I could tell she meant it. I wished I could help her.

Sometimes, Mommy would get mad at me. She would yank on my leash or push me aside when I was being "too much." In all fairness to her, I was being aggressive and not listening to her in those moments. I wanted to be in charge. I was Wolf! Why couldn't anyone see that? I wrestled with all the big dogs, I jumped higher than any of them, I even got into a few fights with dogs that were talking nonsense. I was not scared! I was strong! *I AM Wolf!*

When I acted aggressively at home, Mommy would get annoyed. She would pick me up and put me in the bathroom with the door closed. There was more room in there than the crate, but I didn't like being closed in. I knew better than to cry. I just sat there and thought about things. I was not put in the bathroom often, only if I tried to bite Mommy or the others, or showed my teeth in anger and growled, or did something to the furniture; *that* was when I would be confined to the bathroom. I always felt bad afterwards. Especially when I tried to bite Mommy. Bear told me to make peace with the humans. He said it was just because I was getting older and wanted to be Alpha that I would act out like that. *Fine!* I had to wait to be freed from the bathroom before I could make peace, though.

On one specific occasion, Mommy was terribly angry with me. When she opened the door to let me out of punishment, she did not say a word. I dashed out of the bathroom but then walked slowly to Mommy and gently put my paw on her. She would not look at me. I put my paw on her again. Nothing. I sat down and looked at her and put my paw on her in repeated pats. Finally, Mommy looked at me. I tilted my head and looked her right in the eyes; I was trying to melt her with my eyes. She let out a breath and showed her teeth a little.

"Oh, Baby, come here!" She held me and kissed me and said she loved me. I kissed her neck and face.

"Mommy, I love you so much. I am sorry."

Funny thing about Mommy—she was not like other humans. She would get mad, and then the next moment she was no longer angry. I saw other humans stay mad for an awfully long time. Not Mommy. For her, she felt sad being angry. She lived each moment and each interaction as if it were completely new, unattached to the one prior. In many ways, she was more dog than human.

That probably was why Mommy could communicate with me well. I could hear Mommy's Animal-Speak, but I was not sure if she always heard me. I asked Bear. He said that it was common for humans to not "hear" others. They were trained to only hear their own spoken languages. I wanted Mommy to hear me. Bear said it would take time. He then asked me about my purpose. I still did not know what it was. He laughed.

"It will show itself to you when you are ready. Keep training."

UGH. I wanted to know *now*. I was frustrated. When I felt

frustrated, I would go under the bed and stay there. It was quieter. I hid some things under there to keep me company: a toy, Sister's sock, Mommy's underwear. That was all I needed. I just wanted to be left alone to figure out my purpose. I heard Mommy say that I was "sulking." Whatever. Let me "sulk." Pfft.

16

DIESEL

I was particularly moody for some time. This searching for a purpose was weighing on my mind. Navigating through this world was hard. I wanted to be free like Wolf, but I also wanted to stay with Mommy. I felt a burning desire to do something useful. I wanted to make a difference. I wanted adventure and stability at the same time.

I heard Mommy come home, but I did not leave my sanctuary. I had brought more things under there and hid them far back to the center of the bed. A shoe, a slipper, more toys, more socks, a treat, and a bone. There was no reason for me to leave. I could stay there for a long time. Except I did have to relieve myself. If I stayed there, the feeling would pass, and I would forget about it. Mommy asked where I was and if either Brother or Sister took me outside. They said they had not seen me. This was true. They hadn't. I had been in my Sanctuary. I heard them call my name, but I just ignored them. Mommy got mad. She was yelling at them. They were supposed to take care of me and make sure I went outside to relieve myself. It wasn't really their fault. I was being stubborn and moody. Now I felt bad. I was not maintaining peace. I was the reason for the yelling!

I came out sleepily and stretched. I wagged my tail. Mommy put my leash on to go out. She reminded me that I had to come out for Brother or Sister so I could go out. I just looked at her. I wondered how long I was under there. My mouth felt dry. I rolled my tongue in my mouth and it made a funny sound. Mommy looked at me and said I had "sticky mouth" because I had not had any water. She let me drink first. It was nice to get water in my mouth. I did not realize how thirsty I was. My stubbornness was not healthy for me, I realized in that moment.

It felt so good to be outside! We walked and walked and walked. The more we walked, the better I felt. Mommy too. She was no longer upset and was shedding her dark cloak. The aggravation and negativity that she brought home was slipping away. I felt my mood improving with each step. There were so many smells and things to explore. I walked over to the spot where I hid my treat a long time ago. I moved things around with my nose. It was still there! I grabbed it and ate it right away. Mommy seemed pleased and said I was a great "hider." While we continued walking, I would glance up at her every now and again. She was looking at me too, showing her teeth gently.

We saw something noticeably big up ahead. *Huge.* I smelled the air and lifted my front paw. Mommy asked me what I saw. It was a dog. An exceptionally large dog! As we approached, Mommy began talking to the human. This dog was called Diesel. He was the biggest Rottweiler Mommy had ever seen. I saw Mommy's mind remember a Rottweiler that she had many years ago. Her name was Roxie. It made Mommy happy and sad to remember her. I wanted to learn more about Roxie, but right now, Diesel had my attention. I did not care that I was smaller than half of Diesel's leg. I went right up to Diesel to say hello. Diesel said hello back and then let me climb all over him. Mommy and the human were talking about us. The other human was impressed with my bravery. That made me feel proud.

As we walked away, Diesel said, "Keep up the good work, soldier!"

Wow! Was I a soldier? I protected my family, I was fast, athletic, strong, and had keen senses. Of course, I was a soldier. I was a good soldier!

Was that my purpose?

17

TRAINING MOMMY

*B*rother and I liked routine. Things could be controlled with a routine. You knew what to expect. Everything had a place. Brother was able to navigate his life with this structure. This also gave him time to think. Because of this, Brother was able to make smart decisions. I understood that about Brother. The power of structure and routine! Sister also had a routine that she liked to a point. She was able to do well with her routine as well; however, her room did not reflect that. That was how I was able to get so many socks from her room. Mommy had a routine too, but she hated it. She needed it to enable her to take care of everything and everybody, but it stifled her at times. Mommy craved adventure. She wanted to see different things and experience life beyond the daily routine. Even when she went away for a week on a work vacation, she enjoyed it because she was able to see new things and rest.

I missed her so much that week. I did not like being apart. Brother and Sister took good care of me, but I was always worried about Mommy. I couldn't hear her thoughts, and I was sure she didn't hear mine. How was I supposed to take care of her and be the soldier I was when she went off like that? As the days passed, I found myself becoming angry with her.

When Mommy came home, I did not look at her. I wanted to make sure she knew that I was not happy about her leaving me. She called me to her, and I walked over with my head turned to the side. No. I would not look at her. I would not give kisses. Mommy kept saying my name.

"Baby! Don't be mad at me. I love you. Come here!" she said.

I was walking very slowly toward her. I would not run to her. My tail started wagging the closer I got to her. *Traitor!* I turned and barked at my tail and nipped at it. *How dare you wag when I was trying to make a point?*

Mommy started laughing, and the sound was so beautiful. I shook my head, jumped on her lap, and gave her kisses, placing my paws on either side of her head.

"I love you, Mommy. I love you so much!" I said to her in Animal-Speak.

To my surprise, Mommy said, "I love you too, my baby!" without using human words.

She heard me! I told Bear immediately that I thought Mommy could hear me. He said that sometimes, when humans are most relaxed, they remember how to use Animal-Speak. This was good news! Now, I must keep Mommy relaxed.

I decided it was time to focus on teaching Mommy Animal-Speak. All I had to do was train Mommy to trust her instincts and believe what she heard. To do this, I would need to pay close attention to her every move. I would listen closer to her human words. I would do everything she thought or said right away. This would help her make the connections needed for Animal-Speak. Eventually, she began to understand that I could see her pictures. From there, I would have to get her to see my pictures. That would be the hard part. It was very frustrating, to be honest. I did not understand why humans would let such an important skill go to waste. No matter how I thought about it, I could not understand the reasoning behind letting Animal-Speak go.

Bear was right. I noticed that when Mommy was the *most* tired it was easiest for her to hear me. That is most likely because her guard was down. I would send extra messages to Mommy at night when she was tired or about to fall asleep. This process took a very long time, but when Mommy did hear me, she grew excited. I believed if I kept at it, Mommy would regain her skill and master Animal-Speak. This was important to me; I believed it would be important in the future as well.

LYME DISEASE

*W*e had a lot of fun together. We were a pack, or as humans say, a family. I got used to the time alone when they were at work or school. I knew that it was temporary, and that when they came home, we would be all together and play, eat, snuggle, and exercise together. It made the time alone bearable.

Mommy always said "Okay, Baby! I'm going to work. Be a good boy, I'll be back. I love you!"

That is how I knew I would be left alone. Mommy, Brother, and Sister would leave. They had their bags and things with them. It was always a flurry of movement followed by silence. Sometimes, Mommy said those words and my skin-siblings remained home. It was called school vacation. It was nice to have company, but I did not get to do my regular things while they were home. I didn't mind. It was okay. A break from the routine was welcomed. I had my sanctuary to go to if I needed alone time. I would go there when I needed to think or talk to Bear in peace. I could not hear him very well when the TV was on loud. So much noise. The vibrations from the TV interrupted the messages. My sanctuary was perfect because most of the noise and vibrations were blocked, and messages would come and go freely.

One morning when I woke up, I felt unwell. My back legs hurt a lot. I tried to shake it off and thought maybe I spent too much time in the Sanctuary. I got up and tried to stretch, but it hurt too much. When I walked, my movements were not fluid or easy. I walked over to Mommy so she would be able to help me. Mommy noticed right away. She rubbed my legs and back and asked me what was wrong. I felt Mommy's heart grow heavy and tried to pretend I was okay. I thought I should not have walked over to her so slowly and in pain. She noticed though. Mommy watched me as much as I watched her.

I heard Mommy tell Brother and Sister that I needed to go to the Vet. She was very worried. Brother walked in his room; he was worried but did not know what to do. This was outside of his routine. Sister looked worried too. Mommy took me to the Vet right away. They stuck a needle in my leg and took some blood. I did not like that. It hurt a bit. They needed my blood to do some tests. I was very brave. I did not even cry when they put that sharp pointy needle in my leg. I remembered the first few times I was stuck with a needle. I whimpered and yelped. I was a little baby then. I was not a baby anymore.

The Vet told Mommy that I had Lyme disease. Mommy had water in her eyes. She was worried and sad. That made me sad and a little worried too. I asked Bear what Lyme disease was. He told me that a bug bit me and put a sickness inside me. That was why my legs hurt. He did not seem too worried. He said it would be okay. It was not my time, yet. Good. Stupid, chattering insects!

It turned out that Mommy was an excellent healer. She gave me the medicine the Vet provided, and she massaged my legs and gave me extra love. I started to feel better and enjoyed the extra attention. Mommy spoke to me more. She told me that I had to get better. She needed me. I concentrated on my legs and pictured myself being healthy and strong. Bear was also sending healing messages to me. When we went back to the Vet, I got a clean bill of health. Sort of. I would always be susceptible to certain things now because of the Lyme disease. But for now, I was doing great. Mommy was so happy. We went to the park for a nice walk. Ahhhh! Health is so important!

I was ready to get back to training Mommy and practicing my jumping again.

PRESENTS

*D*ays and nights flowed into each other. Routines were broken up with fun activities. I grew older; everyone did. Time passed and yet, in some ways, time stood still. We were a family, and there was comfort and peace knowing that. Everyone had a place in the family. Mommy was the leader. She was a good leader. She knew more than us, and even when we didn't listen, we knew she was right. Sometimes, rarely, Mommy made a mistake. She always admitted it and apologized. That is the sign of a great leader. Brother, Sister, and I were always thankful even when we didn't show it. I liked to show it more because I knew Mommy needed that, but also because I loved to show her. It did not matter if I got a treat or not, although they were tasty. What mattered was that my tail wagging, kisses, snuggles, and company made Mommy happy. That was all I needed to know. Showing and giving love also lifted my moods, too! Funny, when you give love, you receive it back ten-fold!

In between the routine days, we would do special things. Driving to visit Grandma, long walks, and occasional fancy dinners were just some things to look forward to. Mommy also made certain days special. It seemed like Mommy liked to make days feel special and found a way to create them, even if it wasn't normally a big deal.

For example, Mommy liked to change the apartment by hanging up things that made it look different. When the leaves started changing, Mommy would put up things that looked like cobwebs and spiders and pumpkins. I knew not to touch them. I would just nudge them with my nose to make sure they were not alive. Sometimes, I would growl and bark at the bigger things. Mommy and Sister always laughed when I did that. I wouldn't stop barking and pouncing in front of them until Mommy got up and said "It's okay, Baby. These are friends," and she would pet them like she did me. When she did that, I stopped. I understood these things were not a threat.

In the cold months, Mommy had more things around. She called them Snow People. I tried to bite them thinking they were intruders. Mommy went to each one, petted them, and said "They are okay. They are our friends." I did not bother with them again. I understood. Every year these "friends" came to visit. They seemed to stay for a long time. I did not mind. When Mommy went to work, I felt like I had company.

During this time, Mommy would also bring a tree inside the house. A *tree!* An outside, real life *tree!* It smelled so nice I crept over to smell it. Mommy told me not to relieve myself on the tree. This was a bit confusing. *It's a tree, and I always relieve myself on trees.* But I learned quickly that this was a special tree, not one for relieving oneself.

The tree was incredibly special and represented a season of love and giving. Brother, Sister, and Mommy put special things on it to show how special it was. These ornaments and lights lit up the whole room, filling it with sparkling light and joy. She put a lot of boxes and things wrapped in paper and told me they were presents. I knew what that meant. I loved presents! I had already learned that presents were fun, and we got them toward the end of the Snow People's visit. Sometimes there were a few, sometimes many. It was always fun to open them.

Mommy also had big socks hanging up. I even had a special hanging paw-sock that was filled with treats. We all had so much fun pulling out the surprises from inside them. My favorite present of all the presents was a sheep. This was never inside the stocking but under the tree. It was bigger than me, but I carried it everywhere and was able to lift it onto Mommy's bed with a little practice. Sometimes she would come in and say "Oh, dear! Little Bear, that's not appropriate!" But then she would laugh. Mommy gave me sheep all the time. She called them my "girl-friends." I had a lot of girlfriends.

We also received presents on our birthdays. I had a birthday too. Mine came in the early Spring; it was still a bit cold and very rainy. That was how I knew my birthday was coming. My birthday celebrates the day my Mom brought my body into the world. I thought of Mom often and Angel too. I knew I would see them again someday. I just did not know when. Until then, I was incredibly happy with my human family.

Presents came in different shapes and sizes. Sometimes they were things we could eat, sometimes things to wear, like a new sweater or a new necklace. Often, they were new toys. I had a lot of toys. I always picked a favorite toy and walked around with it in my mouth, showing everyone that I had captured it. I do not think they understood what I was saying. It did make them laugh to see me walk around with it in my mouth. Humans find the strangest things funny. I didn't laugh when they carried around their things. I got annoyed at this sometimes and would just stop walking and stare at them with the toy in my mouth. I could stand there staring at them for minutes. Then I would walk away slowly for emphasis and go to my Sanctuary. I heard them laughing as I left. Pfft.

Mommy liked to have fun. Every now and then, she would put music on and just move her body in rhythm to the music. She called it dancing. Sometimes she would hold my front paws, and we would dance together. Other times, she would pick me up and we would dance slowly hugging each other. I liked doing that. I could feel her heartbeat, and she kissed my face. Sister did the same thing with me. Mommy and Sister were very much alike. Brother would just look at us and shake his head. I could tell he was happy though. I was happy too. I wanted it to be like this forever.

I also helped Mommy with her work. She would sit at the screen and move her fingers across the board making clicking sounds. She would stay there like this for hours. Sometimes she would get up and stretch and make a grunting sound. I knew this meant she was getting tired or annoyed at the work. But she would always sit back down and start again. When I sensed she was getting particularly annoyed, I climbed onto her lap and stared at the screen. I did not know what it said or what I was doing, but Mommy said I was helping her. I felt her heartbeat relax and sensed she felt calmer. She kissed my head and petted me in between moving her fingers across the board. I stayed there as long as I could and then jumped down. I liked helping her. Mommy showed me her teeth and then continued working.

One night, when Mommy worked particularly late, I went to bed and waited for her to join me. I didn't like being alone in bed; I didn't like her working so late. I jumped down off the bed and walked into the room and stared at her. I was sending her messages to go to bed. It worked! Mommy got up and said, "You're right, Little One. It is time for bed. Enough is enough!"

In a way, I gave Mommy a present in these moments. The gift, or "present," was *encouraging the pause*. My calling her to bed forced her to stop working and pause so she could rest.

After turning off the lights and going to the bathroom to brush her teeth and do her night routine, she would climb into bed and exhale. I loved bedtime. I snuggled with Mommy until she fell asleep. Then softly I would move to the end of the bed to get comfortable.

I did not sleep soundly like Mommy. I slept, but it was a different type of sleep. I was partially awake, listening to sounds and feeling vibrations. Being a Security Guard was a full–time job. It made me feel proud to protect my pack, my family.

DEPARTURE 1

*M*ommy was crying. It was the worst sound in the world. The worst feeling. I felt sad and sick watching her cry. I went up to her and kissed her face. The water on her cheeks was salty. She hugged me and cried. She asked that I never leave her. Why would I leave her? *Never!*

The reason for Mommy's sadness was that Brother was leaving. He found his Life's Purpose! He was extremely excited. How lucky to know your life's purpose! He joined the Air Force, I heard Mommy say on the phone. He was going far away for training. Mommy would not be able to see him or call him or anything for a while. Brother was going to be a solider just like the brother in Wolf's pack! *Funny how life has a way of repeating itself.*

I was happy for Brother. I also understood that this changed everything in our house. It meant that I was now the Alpha Male. I saw Wolf in my mind and stood up taller. I was in charge now. I would protect my family even more than before. They would be okay, Brother. I was on duty! I watched outside the window and saw Mommy crying and hugging Brother. They hugged each other for a long time. A soldier stepped back and gave them time to say goodbye. I howled a slow, deep, and long howl, expressing love, unity, and a heartfelt farewell. I hoped Brother heard me.

Mommy was not the same after Brother left. She did not cook anymore. She did not laugh. She just sat there and cried. I understood. Mommy felt incomplete. Brother brought some stability to her. His calm ways helped keep Mommy level. Mommy now felt scattered; she felt nervous and scared and lonely. I think she remembered the time long ago when I was Wolf, and Brother left to fight in the war. He left me in charge then too. He left his family then and left them again now. Same situation, different time. Sister felt sad and lost too. She stayed in her room more. Sister had friends, though. People who could distract her. Mommy just had work and us; and now, "us" was one less.

After many days, I brought her my favorite toy and dropped it at her feet. She looked at me and tilted her head.

"I'm sorry, Baby! I've been neglecting you," she said.

She tossed the toy, and I ran and got it. I brought it back to her but held it tight in my mouth.

"Oh! You want to play tug-of-war?" she asked with a laugh.

Now Mommy tried to get it from me. I held on tight. *I am Wolf! I am strong!* Mommy laughed. I was so happy to hear that sound I dropped the toy. UGH! Now Mommy had it, and she threw it again. I ran after it and brought it back. We played like this for a while. When Mommy had enough, she said,

"Okay, Baby. Let's make something to eat!"

Yes! Mommy was going to start cooking again! I ran around in a little circle, so full of joy. Mommy gave me little bits of food while she was cooking. So yummy! Then Mommy did something surprising. She knelt down and put her face to mine and said, "Thank you, my love. You are my best friend. I love you!"

I howled inside. Bear heard me. He said I was doing a great job and was immensely proud of me. I felt like I was big now. I stood taller. I was living up to my Alpha–Male promise. I was a good boy and not a baby anymore. It brought me joy to see

Mommy feeling better. Sister came downstairs and was happy to see her cooking too. Things were getting back to normal, as normal as they could be without Brother in the house.

I curled up on the floor and rested. . . never taking my eyes off Mommy.

21

BOARDING

*M*ommy was bringing me to the Vet to stay over for a few days. I did not like this. I was not asked if it was okay. They just decided to do it. Mommy and Sister were going away to visit Brother. They were very excited about it except they could not take me with them. I wanted to see him too. Why was I not consulted? I was angry and sad. Were they going to leave me here forever? What if they never came back for me? How was I supposed to protect them if I did not go with them?

Mommy was sad to leave me. She promised to come back. Mommy said she was sorry but repeated that she would come back for me and told me to be a good boy. The Vet had large cages in the back. I was placed in one. There were two bowls for water and food. The girls there liked me and gave me kisses, but I had to stay in the cage. The other cages were filled with dogs and cats making noise. The dogs barked constantly. They were complaining and just being annoying. I tried to Animal-Speak with some of them, but it was too noisy, and they were not paying attention.

The days at the Vet were boring. I was let out a few times a day to go outside to relieve myself. There were no long walks like

I was used to taking, just enough time to relieve myself. Then back in the cage. Mommy left me with one of my toys. I snuggled up to it and slept most of the time. The other dogs did not talk to me at first. They were too busy complaining. One dog was sad and just whimpered all the time. I tried to calm her down. When everyone finally calmed down, I told them all about my life with Mommy.

I was surprised to hear that the other dogs did not walk on leashes. They just ran around in their yards like Bear did. I wished I had a yard to run around, but they wished their humans walked them. They said it sounded nice to be able to explore other areas and see other things. Hm. I guessed there was good in each situation. Some of the other dogs here were too sick to participate in our conversation. They just grumbled or slept. I wished them health, like Bear had done for me when I was sick.

I spent a lot of time talking to Bear. He distracted me with stories about his days and the things he saw in the woods. Bear was good company, and I was grateful to be able to talk to him regularly. Bear was always interesting and always had something important to relay. I enjoyed listening to his stories. It was a great way to pass the time.

I tried to send Mommy messages. Nothing. It seemed like she forgot how to listen. I listened to her thoughts, though. She was so incredibly happy to see Brother. I saw a picture of him through Mommy's mind. He looked good. Healthy, happy, and somehow so much more grown-up! Mommy was laughing again. It was nice to see that. Still, I wished Mommy would talk to me. Didn't she remember me? Did she forget about me? I kicked my food bowl with my nose. Stupid bowls. I did not even like this food. Pfft.

22

_____

HOME AGAIN!

I could smell them. They were back! A girl grabbed my leash and my snuggly toy and lifted me out of the cage. She hooked me up to my leash and started walking toward the front of the office. I could not walk fast enough and dragged the girl who held my leash. She tried to pull back on the leash, but I was not having that. This was not a leisurely stroll. I wanted to get to my family! I did not even want to act mad at them. I was so happy they were back! Mommy kept her promise. She came back, just like she always did.

I wagged my tail so hard when I got close to them that I fell on the slippery floor. Everyone who was there laughed, and I did not even care. Mommy and Sister returned for me and I was overjoyed! They hugged me and petted me and gave me kisses. I gave kisses and jumped on them and wagged my tail. I knew I looked ridiculous, but who cared? I did not feel like the big Alpha Male; I felt like a little baby. Funny thing, I was happy to be the baby. I was happy to be *their* baby. I was *happy*!

The ride home was the best ride ever. It was nothing special, but it was the ride *home*, and that made it exciting. I paced in the back and looked out every window. I stuck my head toward the front and kissed Sister and tried to reach Mommy, but she was driving and could not turn her head. They were happy and asked me how everything went. I did not feel like getting into details at that moment. I would share with them later. Right now, I just wanted to enjoy the ride home. When we arrived on our block, I wagged my tail hard. *Yes! It is our home!* I could not wait to investigate and see all my other toys.

I raced up our stairs, taking two and three stairs at a time. Wow! I was quite impressed with my athletic skills. I ran inside and jumped on the couch, leaping through the air and landing in the middle of the couch. WHOOOOOOO! That felt great! I did it again. I was so happy to be home! I ran up the other stairs to Sister's room. I quickly peeked into Brother's room just in case he was there. I knew he wouldn't be. I ran back into Sister's room, and I took a pair of socks and quickly brought it to my Sanctuary. Mommy saw me. She said to me in her mind, "That's okay. Just don't rip them."

Wow! I decided to show her that I heard her. I walked in the room with the socks in my mouth and showed them to both. Then I walked out of the room. Then I walked back to them, showing the socks a second time to make sure they saw me with the unharmed socks. I hid the socks under the bed and left them there for safe keeping.

Mommy opened the back door, and I ran out to the deck. I barked right away. There was nothing there. I was just letting Squirrel know I was back. I looked around and then lay down taking in some sun. There is nothing better than being home. I could tell Mommy felt better. She needed to see Brother and know that he was happy and safe. Although she still missed him, it was less painful.

Life is funny that way. You can miss someone, but you still must continue your days doing your usual things. If you do not live each day, you become sad and sick, and the someone you miss is still not with you. It just makes sense to keep living each day as you normally would, love who is with you and talk to the someone you miss in your mind.

A few days later, I brought the unripped sock back to my sister's room. I was a good boy. I was also learning.

23

ADJUSTMENTS

*L*ife without Brother started to feel normal. We still missed him terribly, but we got used to it. Mommy worked hard at making things feel right. She made time for Sister and me; more than normal. We looked forward to the days that Brother called, and she shared everything that was going on at home with him. He shared his stories with us, too. It made us feel connected to each other.

That is how Life works. Things change and we adjust. What was new becomes normal. What was old becomes a memory. Change is how we grow. When you cannot adapt to change, that is when things fall apart. Life is like a running stream. It keeps flowing, changing direction; it can be calm or rough, but it is constant. A stream will always be a stream; family will always be family. I think of Mom. She will always be my mom; we are connected through time and space. Nothing could ever change that. Mom had to adjust to many changes; so did her pups. So do my humans. Another change was coming. I could sense it.

Mommy did not go to work anymore. She was home working on her computer. She tried to show her teeth, and she made her voice sound happy, but there was a heaviness in her voice. Her eyes were sad and worried. There was tension in the air. When the cloak of fear was especially heavy and draped around her, I climbed onto her lap and asked her to pet me. She always did. I liked the way it felt, the rhythmic motion, light pressure on my body, the warmth of her body, and the feel of her heartbeat. I did not climb on her for me, though. I did it because Mommy needed it. When I was on her lap in those moments, that heavy cloak of fear slipped away. I pictured myself as Wolf pulling it away from her with my teeth, ripping it to pieces and freeing Mommy from its tangled embrace. I was a warrior. I was protecting Mommy from the cloak's evil grip.

We had many nice walks during this time. I enjoyed seeing my friends. I was extremely popular in the neighborhood with both humans and their dogs. Everyone seemed to know my name. Mommy said I was the neighborhood celebrity. I did not know what that meant, but I knew that it made Mommy happy. Two of my friends were not around anymore. Their human said they died. I was sad about that, but I also understood that they were not gone forever. They crossed the Bridge and were in Joy now. I could see them and talk to them with Animal-Speak whenever I wanted. Still, it was different. I didn't want to think about the Bridge. It was not scary; on the contrary, Joy is a wonderful place! I had faint memories of it, and Bear and I discussed it on occasion. However, I knew it meant a big change.

Some changes are more permanent than others. Those changes are hardest to overcome.

Mommy finally went back to work, but this time she was happy about it. She started her own business as a healer close to home. Brother came to visit too! He helped Mommy get things ready for her new business adventure. It was great to see Brother. We had so much fun together. Everything seemed so busy and full of excitement. The energy at home was high and full of promise, until Brother left again. Mommy shed tears and was sad, but "the great sadness" did not last as long. Mommy was doing much better with change. She was strong. She was our constant source of energy and love. Change. Nothing stays the same forever and we learn to adjust.

24

MOVING AGAIN!

he weather was getting colder. We had passed the season of Snow People and the indoor tree. We had plenty of treats and a few presents, but not many this year. Mommy said it was because she just started the new business. It was okay. We had a lot of fun. We visited Grandma and the rest of the family. We sent a big box to Brother, and he called Mommy often. Life was good. Different, but good.

This year, however, Mommy did not bring the boxes of Snow People downstairs. They stayed upstairs. In fact, every day there were more boxes. Every day, Mommy filled a box with something from our home. We were moving.

Everything was being put in boxes. Mommy and Sister were sad about it. They didn't want to leave here. I didn't want to leave here either. I loved this home. I was the ruler of the neighborhood here. I knew everyone and everyone knew me. I didn't like to see our things being packed into boxes. It made me nervous. I tried to stop Mommy a few times by nipping at the box she was using or barking loudly. She just told me stop and kept packing things. Sister had to pack her own room. She was stressed out. Some things she had to leave behind. Mommy took care of everything else, and there was a lot. Packing up Brother's room made her very sad. This had been his home, and now it would not be available to him.

I followed Mommy everywhere, closer than normal. I watched everything that she took and placed in a box or bag. We had a lot of things, and it was hard for my humans to decide what to bring and what to discard.

Decisions. Change. Humans really do make things more complicated than is necessary. The less you have, the less you need to worry about. Animals only have themselves and their family. We do not have things. We just live life and enjoy Life. I tried to tell Mommy that these things did not matter too much.

"Just let them go," I tried to tell her.

We took a short drive in the car. Mommy brought me to the new apartment. It was much smaller than home. I walked around smelling every corner. Mommy took me to the back where there was a small room and lay down on the floor, patting the space next to her for me to lie down with her.

"This is our new room, Baby," she said.

I could see her mind imagining what it would look like once we moved all our things here. I walked around smelling everything again. I heard Mommy walk down the stairs with Sister, and I panicked.

"Don't leave me," I barked.

Mommy called to me and said, "Come on, Baby! Let's go!"

I felt silly when I heard her say this. Of course, Mommy would not abandon me. I don't know why I thought she would. Mommy always came back.

We got back in the car and drove home. It didn't feel like home anymore. The new place did not feel like home either. Everything felt weird. I did not know where to lie down or what to do. I paced back and forth. I stayed close by Mommy. Too close. Her foot bopped me in the head several times.

"I'm sorry, Baby! You are right underfoot!"

I took a few steps back, but I kept my eyes on her and the

humans that were bringing all the big things Mommy could not fit in the car.

I ran inside the bedroom and grabbed my snuggly from underneath the bed. I did not want to leave this behind. Strange. It seemed that my time with humans was making me have attachments to things. I thought about that. Was I becoming a human? I would talk to Bear about this later. I kept my snuggly in my mouth. It made me feel better.

Squirrel was sitting on the railing of the deck. I said goodbye to him. He chattered back a response. He wasn't so bad. I thought I would miss him too. I jumped in the car with my snuggly and checked the seat to make sure my bowls were there. They were, along with Mommy and Sister. I was ready for this change—together.

25

CEDAR GROVE

I made a new friend! Downstairs in our new home there was another dog. Her humans called her Coqui. She was beautiful with black shiny fur. Coqui was much bigger than me, but I think she liked me. We smelled each other and I climbed on her back. We licked each other's faces and ears. Mommy called it "kissing." I liked seeing her. Sometimes, when we were both alone in our homes, we talked to each other. It was comforting to know she was there. She was also a good security officer, like me. We barked at the human that came by every day to drop off envelopes and papers.

Mommy took me out for many walks. There were so many new places to go, I almost didn't mind not being in my old neighborhood; discovering new things seemed like a little adventure. No one knew me here yet. I made sure to pee on every tree and bush so that they could start sensing me. This would make actual meetings easier.

Eventually, I saw other dogs with their humans. I was shy in the beginning. I made friends with all the big dogs first. They were friendlier and not scared of anyone new. The little dogs yelled at me from a block away; I was not sure how to respond. I tried to make friends, but some of them showed their teeth in an angry way, and one even tried to nip me! I watched where they relieved themselves and then immediately relieved myself right on top of their spot. They would learn! They would learn that this would soon be *my* territory. I secretly vowed to take over the neighborhood; I could protect everyone better being in charge.

We saw a lot of deer on our walks. They made Mommy happy. She always said hello out loud to them. They looked at us but did not run. They could tell we were different; we were no threat to them. Mommy continued to talk to them from a distance. I think she was practicing Animal-Speak. I could also hear them talking amongst themselves. They were all female adults with their young. They did trust us but were still cautious. Deer are timid by nature. It was nice to see them, especially the young. I wanted to play with them, but I had my leash on, and their mama wouldn't let them come too close. There were a lot of squirrels and little critters around, as well. I wanted to chase them, but Mommy always pulled the leash back.

"Leave the squirrels alone, Sweetheart," she said to me.

I listened to Mommy and kept walking. Sometimes, I forgot and bolted toward a squirrel who was running up a tree. This made Mommy scream in pain.

"Ouch! Little Bear! You nearly pulled my arm out of its socket!"

I slowed down and looked back at her.

"Sorry, Mommy."

Stupid leash. I could have caught that squirrel if not for this stupid leash. I made a noise that was a combination of a little grunt and an exhale. It was meant to show my disgust. It did. Mommy understood.

"They are just little outdoor creatures, Baby. You can't play with them," she said.

Fine. I walked over to the tree and relieved myself while looking up at the squirrels.

One early morning, we saw a little animal sitting down the block staring at us. It was about my size. We looked a little bit alike. It smelled different though. I started to walk slowly, tip-toeing each step. Then I lifted my front paw and held my tail straight. I sniffed the air. My ears moved in all directions. Mommy was talking to me, but I was not listening. I was concentrating on this creature. This was *not* a dog. We walked toward this creature slowly. It stood up. It was nervous. *Yes! Be very afraid! I am Wolf!* I kept my slinky walk steadily moving toward this intruder. It looked at us again and then ran off onto the field where the deer meet. I walked faster to see if I could see it. It ran quickly under the fence, not disturbing the deer at all. Good. *Leave our friends alone too, you little creature!* Mommy said it was a little fox. The fox was a pretty red color and had a thick fluffy tail. I looked back at my tail and nipped it.

I liked my tail, but I wished it were as fluffy as Fox's tail. Sometimes when I was sad or nervous, I dropped my tail down to hang low between my back legs. When it was low, you couldn't see the hair around it that made it look fluffy. Mommy's voice always made my tail pop straight up and curl. It's almost as if it had a mind all its own. This always made Mommy laugh. I liked to make her laugh. I could not imagine living without hearing Mommy's laugh.

There were other creatures in this new area. I heard them. Some were outside, but there were some inside too. I could not get at them. I heard them though. The outside fliers were very loud. There were many different types of them. I tried to understand them, but I was not used to talking to Fliers. I vowed to practice talking to them when I was alone. They must have important information because they talk constantly.

Bear popped in to ask how I was adjusting. I told him all the stories of the new neighborhood and asked him about the Fliers, or birds, as Bear said they were called. Bear said it is difficult to speak with birds, but not impossible. Only a very clever dog could learn to communicate with the birds. Bear also said that even if you cannot communicate with them, you could learn from them. He advised me to watch their behaviors and listen to the sound of their chirps. Pretty soon, I would be able to understand patterns. I would take Bear's advice, but I also knew I was a very clever dog. I would be able to communicate with them. I would show Bear!

Little by little, the small new apartment felt like home. Mommy was cooking our favorite foods, and we settled in. Our bedroom was small, but I liked it. It felt like a little cave. It was perfect for snuggling and waiting for Mommy and Sister to come home from their day at school or work. I would lie on the bed and gaze out the window, sometimes at the birds and sometimes at Lexi. Lexi was the little dog that lived in the house next door to us. We hadn't formally met, but we exchanged barks and messages. She loved me. She would look up at the house and bark to get my attention. I let out whining sounds so she would know I was thinking about her but could not come out to be near her.

With all the moving and settling in, Mommy and Sister had forgotten about giving me a bath or haircut. I didn't mind. I was glad. I carried the scent of all the outdoor creatures on me. This helped me move through the neighborhood undetected. I could sneak up on creatures if I wanted to surprise them; I could do this *If* I did not have the leash.

One day, Sister chased me around the apartment, and I thought we were playing. I ran and made huge leaps onto the bed and then jumped down again.

She said, "Come here, Little Bear! It's time for your grooming!" Sister's voice sounded different, bringing her voice higher at the end of each sentence. It was suspicious sounding. I was right!

Sister had this thing that hummed in her hand. This was going to be more than a bath. She grabbed me and made me sit still. I listened. I knew better than to move unnecessarily. As she rubbed me with the hummer, I saw my hair fall to the floor. My hair! My beautiful hair! After the haircut, Sister gave me a bath. I still did not like water and tried to move away from it without any success. She poured something on me and started rubbing me. It felt nice, and it smelled nice too. Then came the water again. When all was done, she rubbed me with a towel to get all the water off me. I bolted free from her and ran around the apartment as if I was in a field. I jumped, ran, threw myself down, and rubbed my back on the carpet. I felt great!

Sister put my jewelry back on. I liked wearing it. It was mine. It showed that I belonged to a family. When I walked, you could hear the tags clink. I felt wonderful. I could not wait to go for a walk and show everyone how great I looked!

When Mommy came home, I stood still in front of her. She was tired. She said hello. I didn't move. I was telling her to look at me. She put her bag down and looked at me noticing my haircut.

"Oh, Sweetie! You look so handsome!"

I knew Mommy would think I was handsome. I ran to Sister to say thank you with a quick kiss then ran back to Mommy.

"Can we go for a walk now?" I was leaping up and down.

"Yes, Baby. Let's go for your walk."

26

DEPARTURE 2

As it turns out, there are many different types of departures. Humans have a really hard time with the one called Death. Death seems permanent to them. They do not understand the continuance of Life. Life is fluid, ever moving, ever changing. You do not have to see someone for them to be alive. There is life after Death.

Mommy was crying and wailing and sick to her stomach. Grandma had died. She had crossed over to the other realm, where we cannot see her body anymore. I knew it was coming. I could smell the sickness on her when we visited her the last time. She was old and moved slowly. Her breath carried the disease that would consume her small frame. The last time I saw Grandma, I was extra gentle with her. I let her pet me and stayed by her feet. I licked her feet gently. I didn't bother with the other dogs. My place was near Grandma. Even though Grandma knew she was dying, she was not afraid. In fact, she told me that she was looking forward to leaving. She was not sad to die, only sad to leave everyone behind. Grandma understood Death and Life after Death.

During the last visit, Mommy and Sister were cooking things for her and helping her organize her things in the kitchen. This made Grandma happy. I wondered if she would be able to enjoy the food Mommy prepared. Her time smelled close. Mommy washed her feet and put lotion on them, gently massaging them. It helped Grandma feel better. We all sat outside on the porch so Grandma could feel the sunshine. She looked at all the trees and listened to the birds; she smiled wistfully. The Sun felt good on our backs. It was still a little cool with a gentle breeze, but the Sun was warm and nourishing. When it was time to leave, I gave Grandma extra licks and head leans. I looked into her eyes; we knew we would not see each other again in this life. Mommy and Sister did not know. They hugged Grandma and said they would be back in a few days. We walked toward the door and I turned back to look at Grandma sitting in her chair. She was smiling but looked a little sad.

"It's okay, Grandma. I will take care of Mommy. I will see you soon. Journey well!" I said to her.

We went to the car and drove home.

This reminded me of my days as Wolf. Wolf's physical body died, yet he lived on in this little body of mine. When beings die, a little piece of their soul breaks off and stays with the old body, and the rest of the soul travels until it finds the right new body. This happens so that the physical body of the deceased Being can experience life in the Afterlife. Wolf showed me that place. It is beautiful. Everything that you need is there. Everything good is there. There are no chains, no pains, no sadness, no anger; only beauty and love exist! It is a place called *Joy*.

Grandma understood this, and that was why she was not afraid. Mommy knew this too but did not fully understand. Knowing and understanding are different. Mommy was incredibly sad to lose Grandma. I tried to comfort her. I understood. Most humans cannot talk across space. They rely on seeing and touching. I acted tough, but I also felt sadness when I thought of Mom. Sometimes, even when you know something, it is still incredibly sad to experience it yourself.

Poor Mommy. I heard her words asking Grandma to visit her.

"Send me a sign, let me know you are okay. I miss you! Please visit me."

Her words and thoughts were filled with pain and sorrow; and yet, I was hopeful! *If Mommy was asking for Grandma to visit, then Mommy must know that communication is possible. I will begin teaching Mommy with more determination. I think she is ready.*

Grandma did visit Mommy. She came often sending a Blue Jay or Red Cardinal to grab her attention. She showed herself to Mommy through these messengers. Seeing these birds lifted Mommy's spirits. She often called out to them, saying, "Hello! Thank you for visiting!"

I could feel the burden of sadness lifting away from Mommy at these times. Sometimes, Grandma visited on the days I was alone for a long time. Grandma understood being alone and feeling lonely, and she came to me to offer comfort and company. I loved these visits. They did not scare me; on the contrary, they were most welcomed. Grandma showed me images of her new life. It was just as I knew it would be. Most importantly, Grandma was happy and free from the restrictions of her human body.

Sometimes Grandma would drop a memory into Mommy's head to make her happy and remember good things. Memories. At first, they hurt your heart, but quickly they turn into comfort. Mommy was finding a way to feel the comfort. Little by little she was getting stronger and accepting this change. I could hear her talking to Grandma. Mommy was practicing almost every day. Grandma responded to her quickly. She would send a bird or butterfly right after Mommy spoke to her. This made Mommy certain that it was Grandma and not just her imagination.

One day, Mommy asked me to never leave her. She said she wanted me to stay with her forever, till we were both old. She wanted us to die together. Yes, I would do that. I did not want to leave her either. We would go through this life together. Bear interrupted my thoughts with a message.

"Be careful, Little One. You shouldn't make promises that you cannot keep."

For the first time, I was angry with Bear. What did he mean? Why would he say that to me? Me and Mommy were meant to be together. I picked her and my family on purpose. My entire voyage was so that we would be together again. How dare he tell me I would not be able to keep a promise to stay with Mommy forever! I was so angry. I stopped talking to Bear for what seemed to be many days. I knew he was still with me; I could feel him watching me.

Bear was a patient teacher. When I finally called out to him, he answered me right away.

"Why did you imply I wouldn't be with Mommy forever?" I asked him.

"You will always be with her, Little One. But remember, time and space travel across all planes. Humans do not fully understand that. She cannot see how you will always be together, even after physical death. Pick your messages carefully," he said.

I knew what he meant. I also knew he was right. However, I wanted to stay in the physical body with Mommy forever. I would do my best to make that happen. After all, I could do whatever I put my mind to, couldn't I?

I smelled roses in our bedroom. Mommy did too. Grandma always wore Tea Rose perfume. Mommy looked around and smiled. Grandma was here.

27

ROAD TRIP!

*J*t was the season of the Snow People again. Everyone came out and filled the little apartment with joy and excitement. There was a teeny little tree in the corner decorated with lights and ornaments. Underneath the table the tree stood on, there were many presents of all shapes and sizes. This year, things were a little different. Mommy and Sister were packing clothes in their travel bags. I grew excited and then thought of the big cage at the Vet. I hoped I would not have to go there.

I started acting excited, making little leaps and bounds and carrying my snuggly to and fro. I was hoping that this behavior would be cute and charming and perhaps show Mommy I was a good traveler. Mommy pulled out a small travel bag and started to fill it with my things. Some food, treats, my vitamins, a sweater, and a toy. This either meant I was going with them or she was sending me away. My belly did a little flop. I couldn't eat. I stayed close to Mommy and tried to look even cuter than normal, changing my expression to resemble a puppy.

Then they began to bring all the presents downstairs, filling the car with them. Mommy also put treats and food and water inside the car. I peeked inside the car as she packed and organized everything. There was a space in the back surrounded by all our things for me! Mommy showed me her teeth. Yes! We were going on a road trip! I loved road trips! I spun around chasing my tail in excitement.

"Okay, in the house, Little One. We are not leaving yet!" Mommy said.

I ran up the stairs, stopping after every few steps to make sure she was coming up too. Yes, she came upstairs and got ready for bed. Good. I made sure to snuggle close to her. I was practically lying on top of her with my whole body, just in case she had any weird ideas to leave without me. We got up early the next morning before the Sun even rose. I was full of energy, but Mommy and Sister were sluggish. We all got into the car and were ready to go. I was excited! We were going to see Brother.

The road trip was fun. I looked out the window and saw things moving past us. We stopped every so often to relieve ourselves. I did not like these stops much because there were so many trucks. I kept my ears back and crouched low to the ground, moving as fast as I could to the nearest tree. Mommy and Sister laughed at me and called me a little baby. That was embarrassing. I must try to be braver.

I slept in the car sometimes. It was an awfully long drive. I remembered a long drive when I was a puppy. Back then, we were heading north. This trip, we were heading south and west. I hoped Mommy was not bringing me back. My tail dropped and I growled at it. She would never bring me back. Don't be silly! I asked Bear what he thought, just to be sure. Bear just laughed and said I needed to relax. Mommy had proven herself loyal and kind. She would not return me. Of course, I was being silly. I curled up and slept some more. It was nighttime now. Mommy stopped the car. We went into a little room that had two beds. I ran in looking for Brother. He was not there. I was confused. *Where was Brother? Where were we?* Mommy only removed some of our things from the car and left the rest packed neatly, locking the car door with the familiar "beep" sound. Sister threw herself on one of the beds. I jumped onto the other and then leaped onto her bed. It was fun. I did that many times, stretching my body straight as I propelled off one bed and then landed on the other. Sister and Mommy watched in amazement and laughed.

We ate some food and then lay on the beds watching TV. When Mommy took me outside to relieve myself, I smelled something familiar in the air. Not in the room with two beds, but *here*. The trees, the air. . . all smelled familiar. I was here before, but when? When back inside, I lay on the bed facing the door. I had to make sure we were safe. I was always on duty. As they relaxed, I wondered why we were in this strange but familiar place.

When the sun rose, we got back in the car. Mommy and sister seemed extremely excited. I got excited too but not sure why. We drove so many hours again. We made stops to relieve ourselves and we ate a little in the car. There was a growing sense of familiarity. I could smell it. This was where I lived as a newborn puppy. I smelled harder and faster. Maybe I could smell Bear! I asked Bear where he was at that moment. He was resting in the home where he lived. He did not think I was going to visit, but we talked together for a while; I was telling him all the things I was seeing and smelling. He was excited for me. I wished I could see him again, nose to nose. I wished Mommy could meet Bear.

We were off the highway with all the trucks. This was a new place. The window in the back was open a little, and I stuck my nose close to the opening so I could smell better. I was not sitting down anymore; this was too exciting to sit still. I could tell we were close to our destination. I smelled Brother in the air. After a few more turns, Mommy turned the car into a driveway right in front of nice–looking house. I could see Brother! I was so excited to see him. I stood up tall, and my tail was wagging quickly. *Let me out! Let me out!*

The car doors flew open, and we all jumped out at the same time. Mommy jumped on Brother and hugged him tight. Sister said hello casually but with excitement. We met a new human, and there was also a dog there. My brother had a dog! Hm. This bothered me a little. I was the dog of the family. Me! Did he forget about me? They called the dog Philip. He was all white. Mommy and sister loved him right away. It was easy for them. As head of security, I needed to investigate this dog before I decided if he was okay. Philip. Hmpff.

I took a hesitant smell of him. He seemed okay, but it was too soon to tell. I walked past him looking at him sideways. I did not have my leash on, but I stayed close to Mommy anyway. I tried to say hello to Brother, but Philip got in the way. Oh! He didn't know who I was. He didn't realize that I knew Brother *first*. I walked away to relieve myself but never took my eyes off him. We all went inside with our belongings and put things in the different bedrooms. Brother had an inside tree too! The presents were placed under the tree along with the other presents already there. No Snow People though.

This home was so much bigger than where we lived. Brother also had a big yard. Wow! I could run around and play whenever I wanted. Everyone went outside, and Philip ran down the stairs with a thump to run around the yard. I followed but not too close to Philip. I kept my eyes on him. He ran back and forth along the fence barking and barking. There were dogs on the other side. Why were they barking so much without using Animal-Speak? Weird. I found this behavior very suspicious. I glanced up at Mommy, and she was showing her teeth. She was happy. She gave me the motion to run, and I took off running around the yard. My foot caught in a little hole, and I tripped. I tried to pretend it didn't happen, but they all saw. Not one of my best moments. Not like when I was running fast as a puppy. This was just embarrassing. I just walked around the yard after that.

We had a great time at Brother's house. Mommy and Sister cooked a lot, they played games, everyone showed teeth and laughed. It was nice to see everyone together and happy. It reminded me of when we all lived together in the first apartment.

There were so many presents to open this year! In between opening presents, I ran around in circles and jumped on Mommy or Sister. I wasn't sure what to do with myself. I was having fun, but I still wanted to figure out Philip. He was an interesting type. He was always happy. Nothing seemed to faze him. Even when he was outside barking, there wasn't any real purpose there. He just barked to bark. Sister laughed and said Philip was "vacant upstairs." Mommy laughed. She said, "Poor Philip!" Philip just wagged his tail, and everyone smiled and petted him.

One day, Philip and I had a fight—well, sort of. He was trying to play, but I wasn't in the mood. I growled and nipped at him. He walked away and didn't do anything. Nothing. Sister said he was dopey. He was not a warrior. He just wanted to play and explore. He was happy just watching everything. He was happy running and eating and being among people. I could tell that he didn't have too many past experiences. Everything was new to him. He was a young soul. I felt bad about my behavior and lay down; I just looked at everyone with my eyes shifting between them. Mommy said I was being jealous. I was not sure what that meant, but I knew what I felt. I felt like Mommy and Sister and Brother should only love me. I wanted all the attention. I wanted all their love. Jealousy. It did not feel nice. It ruined everything. I should have known better. I knew humans could love many beings at the same time. After all, I loved many humans; why was I having a hard time accepting that they could love many dogs? I vowed to be nicer to Philip. At least I would try.

I ran around the yard with Philip on the next day. He tried to play with me, and I let him for a few minutes. He listened to me. He knew I was older and was beginning to understand that I was Wolf. He was not so bad after all. It was a fun day with Philip. Of course, it was our last day here at Brother's house. I was sorry that I wasted so much time being jealous. Bear told me I learned an important lesson.

"Do not waste time on foolish negative emotions because time is fleeting. Enjoy each moment," he said.

Bear was always so wise. I was grateful to have him around me, helping me navigate life. I felt incredibly lucky.

We were back in the car with all our things and a few less presents. There was more room in the car for me, but Mommy still put pillows and things in the back seat to protect me from falling all over the place. She said it was for my safety. We were heading back north. The trip didn't feel as exciting going back, but I still enjoyed the ride. The routine was the same. We stopped every now and then, only this time it was more leisurely. We stayed in another room with two beds when it was dark. We all slept well, and no one rushed to get up. When it was light out, we got back in the car for another long day of driving. The air was starting to feel colder. Finally, we arrived back home.

I was excited to be home and to see Coqui. She greeted me enthusiastically. Nothing much happened while I was away, according to her. She didn't have much to report. She told me she barked extra loud at the guy who brought envelopes every day. I told her she did a good job. She licked my face, and I licked her ears. My first walk being home was nice. It was nice to see all the deer. I had enjoyed running loose in the yard at Brother's place, but I really did enjoy walking with Mommy. We took a nice long walk at night. There were a few new smells, and I relieved myself on them. Everyone must know I was back. This was my neighborhood, after all.

It was great to see all our things in the apartment too. The Snow People were still out, and they did not disrupt anything while we were away. I jumped on the bed and the couch and ran back and forth. It made me happy to be around all our things. Home. This little apartment finally felt like home.

It was at that moment that I decided something. Sometimes, when you leave the familiar and then return to it after an adventure, you feel better about it. You see it differently than before you left. I felt good about my life. I loved my things. I loved the neighborhood. I loved the familiar. Bear called it "appreciation." I curled up and slept. I dreamt of Brother and Philip. It was great to see them. It was great to be home. Life was good.

28

SICKNESS

Something was wrong. I was not feeling well. My insides hurt, and I felt so thirsty. No matter how much I drank, I still felt thirsty. Mommy looked at me with worry. She knew something was wrong. She gave me extra snuggles and cuddle time. Mommy gave me food that I tried to eat. It did not help; instead, I threw up twice. This made her more worried.

We got in the car. We were going to the Vet. Mommy talked to me on the ride. She said not to worry. We were just going to find out what was wrong. I could tell Mommy was worried. She felt anxious. I remembered this place. I relieved myself by the little tree in front of the building. This was my tree. I always marked my territory on this very tree. I remembered all the humans inside. They were nice and remembered me, too. They always showed their teeth and said hello to me in high voices; but they always pricked me with something, too. I did not like that part. I was feeling tired, even though it was early in the day and I had not done anything. One of the girls had to carry me inside because I refused to walk. I was able to walk, but I did not want to be pricked. I definitely did not want to be left there.

After we saw the doctor, Mommy and I went home. Nothing changed by going to the Vet. I didn't feel any better. I still felt sick. I drank more water and lay down. Mommy kissed the top of my head and petted me. She was holding her phone more than usual. There was a sense of waiting. I was too tired to talk to Bear. I closed my eyes and fell asleep.

Mommy got a call, and she started crying. Her crying woke me up. She did not say much on the phone but kept looking at me, covering her mouth when she spoke into the phone. She was trying to hide something from me. She did not want me to see her crying. I could see it though. I could feel it. I lifted my head to better hear her thoughts. We had to go back to the Vet.

More pricks with needles. There was a new doctor there. She was genuinely nice. I liked her a lot. After being pricked with needles, we sat in the main room and waited. The nice doctor came out after a while and brought us back inside. She was talking while petting me. Her voice sounded nervous. Mommy was crying. She did not try to hide it this time. I wished I knew what was going on. I didn't understand what was being said. I did not understand the messages inside Mommy's head. Mommy was scared. She kept looking at me. She was listening to the doctor but trying to talk to me at the same time, but her messages were scattered. What I understood, I didn't like. Neither did Mommy. The doctor took me from Mommy and brought me into the back area. This was not where I stayed the last time. This time I was in a room all by myself. There was a large crate. A girl stuck me with something in my leg and then attached it to a soft long tube that was connected to a sack that hung above me. Oh, boy. I was sick. Very sick. Mommy told me that she would come back. I was scared. I was alone in the room inside a big crate with the tube and sack.

Bear stayed with me. He talked to me and told me to be brave. He told me stories about his day to distract me. I tried to listen, but I was so tired and weak. I curled up in a corner and tried not to get tangled in the long tube. I looked up at the sack. The liquid was dripping slowly into the tube. It did not help my mouth feel less dry.

I slept a lot. People came in and out all day to check the tube and the sack. They touched me and tried to sound happy. No one took me outside. I was expected to relieve myself on the paper in the crate just like a little puppy. They cleaned the crate every day even though there wasn't much to clean. They tried to get me to eat, but I didn't want anything. The food was not tasty, and my insides hurt too much. My mouth was dry. It felt like my tongue would stick to the top of my mouth. The girl put fresh water in a bowl next to the bad tasting food. I finally drank the water eagerly then curled up again and slept.

Mommy came to visit me every day. She brought me food treats and told me I had to eat. She hugged me and tried to feed me. She was crying. When Mommy visited, I was able to come out of the crate. She sat on the floor, and I sat on her lap. Sometimes, she had to lift me onto her lap because I was too weak to do it myself. Even though I lay down a lot to sleep, it was not a good sleep. I could hear the other dogs talking. They were wondering who was in the Sick Room. I supposed that they were talking about me. I didn't bother to answer them. I just wanted to go home. When I sat on Mommy's lap, she sang songs to me and petted me. She also put something on me that smelled nice, like flowers and herbs. It made me feel calm. Before I was put back in the crate, Mommy lay a nice little blanket with my snuggly from home inside the crate. That was nice. Something from home. I wanted to go home. Every day before Mommy ended our visit, she said the same thing. "You have to eat, Baby! If you want to come home, you must eat. Please, Little Bear. You cannot leave me. I need you."

Leave you? Was that what she thought? That I was trying to leave her? I did not understand what was happening with my body, but I knew I didn't want to leave her! I took a bite of food and headed weakly toward the door.

"See, Mommy? I ate! Let's go home!"

She smiled a little at the knowledge that I understood her

but said, "No, Baby. You must eat a lot. You are too skinny and weak. I'll be back. I love you!"

I felt like I was crying inside. I flopped on top of my snuggly and exhaled.

I was in the Sick Room inside the crate for a long time. It was scary. The other dogs outside this room were yelling and crying. I wanted to go home. I wanted to be with Mommy. She needed me! She told me she needed me. Sister came to visit too. She looked worried. She never cried like Mommy did, but I could tell she was sad inside. I had to get better. Who was going to protect them? Who was going to help them feel better? I curled up in the cage and thought about Wolf. Wolf was strong and healthy. Wolf was smart. *I am Wolf*, I told myself. I stood up and ate some of the bad–tasting food. Bear was encouraging me.

"Eat the food, Little One. Drink the water. You are strong. You can do it," he said.

Mommy came back as promised. The doctor told her that I ate a bit better. She let Mommy take me outside to relieve myself. It was nice to be outside and smell the fresh air. The breeze felt good on my face, and I could hear the birds singing. We were not allowed to walk near my tree, but only in the back close to the Sick Room. After a few minutes, we went back inside. Mommy sang to me some more and put more nice–smelling oil on me. The next day when Mommy visited, the doctor said I could go home! She had a bunch of those sacks and some needles to bring home, along with medicine for me. Before we left, the Vet showed Mommy how to do everything. I was not completely better, and there would still be needle pricks, but I did not care. I was going home! I wasn't going to leave them or abandon my duties. I made a promise, and, just like Mommy, I kept my promises.

Several days after returning home, I started feeling better. Mommy was a great healer. I listened to her and ate the medicine because she covered it in peanut butter. I loved peanut butter. Sometimes, when I was not in the mood for peanut butter, Mommy called on Sister to make me take the medicine. Sister did not play around. She grabbed my face and shoved the medicine in my mouth. I had no choice but to swallow it. Sister was tough when necessary, but I knew it was because she loved me.

Mommy pricked me in the neck and sang to me while I was attached to the tube with the sack of liquid. We did that in the morning and at night. It was not too bad. Mommy was good at it. Her humming distracted me too. I felt myself getting stronger. I began to eat more and put on some weight. This made Mommy happy, so I ate as much as I could. When we went back to the Vet, the doctor said everything looked better. I was stable. Some permanent damage to my kidneys, but stable. I had to relieve myself more often, so Mommy took me out as much as possible. The walks were good. Some were short and some long. Mommy took me on an adventure once a week to my favorite park. We walked in the woods and around the pond. It was fun seeing different animals and meeting friends. I was still on medication, but it was okay. Mommy made a new routine, and I knew just when to take them. She made me special food as a treat sometimes. It was always delicious.

"Good job, Little One! You are strong and smart! I am proud of you!" Bear said.

I felt proud. I felt loved. Mainly, I felt happy to be home with Mommy and Sister.

29

CABOT

*W*e went on another long road trip. We were going to visit Brother again. I knew for a while that we were going. The minute Mommy and Sister started packing things, I knew. I was so excited. I even helped pack my things. I grabbed my snuggly and put it near the bags. Mommy had my suitcase filled with the usual things plus my medicine. I ran up and down the stairs when they packed the car at night. I thought we were leaving at night, but then we came back upstairs for bed. Sleeping was hard. I was too excited. Mommy had a hard time sleeping too. She played special sleep music to help us. It helped a little. When we finally got up, it was still dark outside. The birds were not even chirping yet.

We walked around the apartment to make sure we had everything. Sister grabbed her pillow and went to the car. I knew what to do. I jumped right into the packed car with my snuggly and waited to go. I was not as afraid of the trucks this time. I stuck my nose close to the window to smell everything. We were going south. I could smell it in the air. We made regular stops to stretch and relieve ourselves. I remembered the trees from when we stopped last time. I made sure to relieve myself on them. I liked sending messages to the other animals telling them I was there; I also did it so that I knew how to come back in case we were lost. I wondered why humans could not smell as well as dogs. It was sad, really. You could tell so much from the air and trees. They held stories and information. The ride did not seem quite as long this time, maybe because we had done it before, and it was more familiar.

When we got to Brother's house, I saw Philip. I was awfully glad to see him. I ran up to him to say hello. He remembered me too. He was very happy to see all of us! We all hugged and sniffed and gave kisses. My pack was back together! That was the best feeling. I felt so happy! Then from behind Philip a little teeny dog came running our way. Who was this? What was going on here? Mommy and Sister made a high–pitched sound of excitement when they saw him. I hesitated. I wanted to find out about this little creature who seemed to come out of nowhere.

The little black fluffball was called Milo. He was so small. I looked huge next to him. Milo was very jumpy and bouncy. He seemed to be everywhere at once. Philip and Milo were great friends, and this made me feel like an outsider. This was supposed to be *my* time with Philip. I was going to become great friends with Philip this visit. Why was Milo here? I started to feel that sick feeling I had last visit. Jealousy. I heard Bear talking to me.

"Little One, remember the lesson you learned last time. Do not waste time feeling bad. Enjoy each moment."

Sigh. Yes. Bear was right. I would try.

Mommy and Sister loved Milo and Philip. I let them have time with them, but it did bother me a little. I wondered if they loved Milo and Philip more than me. Mommy called me over and I jumped on her lap. She told me she loved me the best and said I was her best friend. She told me to have fun. Was Bear talking to Mommy? They seemed to be saying the same thing. Hm. Maybe I should listen. They were both wise.

Everyone slept on Mommy's bed: Philip, Milo, and sometimes me. When I got annoyed, I would go to Sister's bed. She liked that. I did too. I felt closer to Sister. I realized that I could love Mommy and still spend time with Sister. Interesting. You could love many without taking away from either.

Milo kept eating my food and drinking my water. He would not let me eat his food or drink his water, though. He was not a good sharer.

"He's just a baby," Mommy said.

I must be patient. I gave him a few low growls to remind him that I was Wolf. Both Philip and Milo listened. We all got along very well after that. It seemed I was their leader even though this was their home. I liked that idea. A leader. Our time at Brother's house was fun! It somehow made me feel more confident. . . and older.

30

I WAS NOT PERFECT

$\mathcal{B}$y now, I bet everyone thinks I was the best dog in the world. I would like to think so, too. Mommy always said that I was, but she loved me and was blind to my faults. To be completely transparent, I would like to take time to review some of my bad behavior. It is only fair, and there really is no point in hiding it!

After all, every experience makes us into who we are and brings us either a step closer to or further from our life's purpose. It is part of life. Part of each of us. Everything is important. How we react to events is more important than the event itself. So here it goes!

I liked to steal Sister's socks and underwear. I took them and hid them under the bed. Then, when I knew it was safe, I ripped them to pieces. I sometimes took Mommy's underwear too, but she stopped getting annoyed with me about it, so I do not bother taking her things. Sister would get mad and stomped around, yelling, so I kept taking her things. It was not that I wanted the items, although I did like to keep Sister's scent close to me for company. I did it because it made her react to me. I wanted more of Sister's attention.

Sometimes, when Mommy tried to get back something I

took, I bared my teeth and growled at her. I even nipped her hand a few times. I felt the most bad about that. I do not know why I did that. It was as if I lost control of my mind for that moment, and thought I was in the wild protecting my things. Mommy would get angry and not pet me. On one occasion, she was so angry with me for hurting her hand that she would not even look at me. As she was lying on the bed reading, I came up and gave her my paw. She refused. I tried again. She refused again. I tried to get on top of her, but she moved so that I could not. What was I going to do? I felt awful.

"Mommy, please!"

I lay very flat on my belly and inched my way up to her, slowly. I could see Mommy was peeking at me from under her reading glasses. I crept on my belly until I was up close to her face. Then I stuck my tongue out and licked her face. Slow licks. Mommy knew that slow licks meant "I love you so much!" That did the trick. Mommy laughed and picked me up onto her belly. She kissed my face and petted my back. I rested my head in the curve of her neck and stayed there a long while. I listened to her heartbeat. Mine was beating hard on top of hers. Our heartbeats matched each other after a while. I felt peaceful.

An embarrassing confession is that I had a few accidents in the house. In my defense, it was when I was sick. I felt bad though. I was not a baby. It was embarrassing to me. I tried to hide it but there were no leaves in the apartment to cover it up. The floor was hard and would not move. I tried though. Mommy never got mad at me. She knew it could not be helped.

"It's okay, Baby. I know you don't feel well," she said.

Still. . .

As I mentioned before, I am the great Protector of the house. I took my job very seriously. Sometimes, too seriously. Sister had friends come over sometimes, and even though I knew who they were, I still barked and lunged at them. *I am Wolf! I am in charge!* Sister would get embarrassed and annoyed and yell at me to stop. I did not stop. I barked more. Then I would get sent to the bedroom and be locked inside. As usual, I stopped barking and just lay down. I should have stopped when she asked. Wolf always knew when to stop.

Stopping bad behavior was especially hard when it came to food. I loved food. I never ate just to eat. I managed to keep my slender weight my entire life. Good food, exercise, and rest. That is the key. Yet, when my family ate, I wanted to taste their food. I stared at them and shook my whole body. This annoyed Sister very much.

Mommy would say, "Stop, Little Bear! You have to wait."

I would listen to Mommy, but I never listened to Sister. She was not the leader. I didn't want to listen to her. I was the Alpha Male. She was supposed to listen to me! I wanted food, and she was not complying. If we were in the wild, Sister would be punished severely for not listening to me. We were not in the wild, however, and I *was* supposed to listen to Sister, because she was Human, not Dog. I didn't agree with these rules; they went against nature. Yet, they were the rules I had to live by, and I felt bad about annoying Sister.

Mommy and I had a lot of friends we saw on our walks. One day, we were talking with Harry and his human. The human was talking too much, and I just wanted to keep walking. There were other dogs to see, other animals, and I wanted to pee on a specific tree I had been thinking about. So, since no one was listening to me, I walked calmly over to Mommy and relieved myself on her foot. Yes. I did that. Mommy was shocked. I was too, to be honest. I cannot explain why I did that. I was just as confused as everyone. We started walking right after that, so everything worked out the way I wanted. Except Mommy's sneaker had pee on it and she was annoyed and embarrassed. I did not think that part through; I was impulsive and inconsiderate.

Over the years, it was known that my room was shared with Mommy. My place for sleeping was on the bed with Mommy. I also stayed there when no one was home. Really, it was *my* bed.

My room. At least that is what I told myself. When Mommy came to bed, I purposely stayed on her pillow on her side of the bed. Every night it was the same thing. Mommy would ask me to move over. I didn't. She tried to squeeze in, but I would not budge. I was surprised to see how heavy I could be, even though I was such a little dog. Every night I gave her a hard time, but in the end, I always moved over, and we snuggled. Sometimes, Mommy would laugh; most times she was tired and got annoyed. I wish I didn't give Mommy such a hard time. What was that word used to describe me once? Willful. Yes, I was being willful.

One of my favorite things to do was to pretend that I was in the wild. Whether at home or outside, I would "hunt" for food. This always led me to the garbage, and I would stick my nose inside and grab something out of there. Then I would eat it or tear it apart making a mess. Mommy always got angry and tried to grab the trash from my mouth, but I was fast and ran under the bed with my capture. If it was something from the outside garbage, or loose on the street, I had to eat it right away. I knew I could not get inside with it. This upset Mommy greatly, especially when I would grab a bone and refuse to walk so that I could eat it. Mommy thought it was gross; she also worried that I was eating something bad that would make me sick. I didn't care. I wanted my capture. I did not feel bad about eating the bones; I did feel bad about upsetting Mommy, though.

The last thing to report on my bad behavior involved the Mailman, the one who brings envelopes every day. I carried on every day he came to the house. He seemed okay. He never did anything wrong, but Coqui and I would bark together at him from inside our apartments. I took it too far, though. When we saw him outside on our walks, I still barked and lunged at him. Even when he was across the street, I let him know that I saw him, and he was not welcome. Mommy would wave at him, and he would say hello, shaking his head at me. Whatever. *She is my*

Mommy, and this is my neighborhood. GET OFF MY BLOCK!
Sigh. That behavior was not very neighborly.

I do believe that is all I ever did that was bad. It is not too horrible, I don't think. In fact, if I were in the wild, these things would be considered normal. They would be considered great skills for protection, for getting food, and for survival. I was a dog, not a human. Dogs do not have so many rules as humans invented for us. It is simpler for us. Still, I should have behaved a little better, if only to not upset Mommy.

31

LIFE WAS GOOD

*W*hen I turned eight years old, I was at my best. I felt great. I looked fantastic. I stopped most of my bad behaviors or at least modified them. I still stole underwear and socks from Sister, but I did not rip them to shreds. I still barked at the Mailman, but it was different. I just barked to let him know I saw him; I was not yelling for him to stay away. I had settled into everything, and my behavior reflected my maturity. I understood human rules better. The wild animals in the neighborhood knew who I was and respected my position. I was comfortable being alone during the day, and I made friends easily when we were out. I really felt in charge of my life. Life was good.

The routine at home was simple. I enjoyed my alone time and used it to talk to Bear and Lexi. I even tried to talk to Philip, but he was dopey, as Sister said. Mommy did a great job getting home from work to take me out for walks. Sister walked me, too, although there were still times when I stayed under the bed to wait for Mommy. I liked it in my Sanctuary. I had my things. I could talk to Bear without distraction. I was able to sleep. I was able to hear outside noises as well as inside noises, even from downstairs. I was perfectly positioned to hear everything while under the bed.

The best development had to do with me but affected Mommy. She was getting rather good at Animal-Speak. She had been listening to something from her phone buds that explained to humans how to talk to animals. Since then, she practiced at home. Mommy would be sitting in the living room while I would be in the bedroom, and she would send me a message to bring her a specific toy or to come in to give her a kiss. Sometimes, she would send me messages on our walks. These usually had to do with which direction she wanted to walk. She was always amazed when I responded the way she wanted me to without her speaking human words. Mommy was very diligent in her studies of Animal-Speak. She also practiced talking to Athena, her dog from many years ago. I knew about Athena. She was beautiful. She was a caretaker of other animals. I had not met her yet outside of my mind, but I knew I would eventually.

Every now and again Mommy heard my messages to her. She was unsure they were from me, but she learned to trust them. I became very diligent in helping Mommy with her new skills. I sent her messages all the time. Constantly. There wasn't a moment that I did not send her a message. She did not hear them all, but occasionally, I knew she heard me. Those were great moments. I tried to reward her every time she heard me. I behaved better or did exactly what she wanted or looked up at her so she would understand that I knew she heard me. It was especially important that Mommy grew in confidence regarding Animal-Speak.

I was not sure why at the time, but it would prove to be an especially important tool. I felt a sense of urgency. I spoke with Bear, and he encouraged me to keep working with Mommy. This became my new focus. My purpose was now to help Mommy speak and listen to animals. All animals, not only me. I sent messages to the deer and asked for their help. Of course, they agreed. Such wonderful, gentle creatures. The squirrels were not so agreeable. No surprise there! We would practice without them.

WEATHER

*H*umans track time with a clock and a calendar. Animals track time by the Sun, Moon, and the shifts in weather. As weather changed, it affected how I felt. Some days were beautiful, and I felt great. Other days, not so much. I want to share my experiences regarding weather. Remember, everything is important. Everything affects decisions and life, which ultimately, affect your Purpose.

Summer was great for the most part. I didn't like when the air was thick and heavy though. It made me feel sluggish. The ground was so hot and hurt my paws to walk on it. I learned quickly to walk on the grass; it was much cooler. I threw myself on the grass and rolled on it to cool off. In the mornings, the grass would be wet with dew. That was especially refreshing.

I liked to lie inside the apartment in spots where the sunlight shone. It was easy to rest there. I could feel the warmth of the sun, and it felt wonderful. Snuggling was hard. We all felt so hot and sticky that after a few minutes Mommy asked me to move over. She was too hot. I liked to snuggle with her anyway. I learned to lie next to her without touching her except for my tail or my foot. She didn't mind that. She was able to pet me without feeling too hot.

I felt thirstier in the summers. I drank more water inside the apartment and outside. I especially liked drinking from the puddles after a rainstorm. This was probably how I got sick in the first place. Mommy did not let me drink the rainwater anymore. She said it had bacteria. I still tried to drink it. Sometimes, I would get close enough to get the tip of my tongue in the water before Mommy pulled up on my leash. She called me willful again for not listening.

Autumn was beautiful. The Sun shone but there was a breeze that carried a coolness with it. This breeze felt good and kept us cool. I could walk forever in the autumn months! The ground was comfortable; I still threw myself on the green grass and rolled around. This time there were many leaves on the grass, which made crunchy sounds under my body. This always made Mommy laugh. I saw her memories of Brother and Sister playing in leaf piles when they were little. Dogs and humans are not so different after all.

There was something different in the air. I would stick my nose up high and smell. The critters were busy running up and down the trees. They were preparing for winter. The trees were also preparing for the winter. They swayed back and forth with the wind and their leaves were changing. Mommy said they were so colorful, but I did not understand this. I could not see colors. I could tell they were different, but I did not see colors the way humans did. By the end of autumn, they dropped their leaves on the ground and began to stand bare, providing me with piles of leaves for playing

Winter was my least favorite time of year. I hated the cold. The snow would fall high enough to reach my belly, and it was hard to walk. Snow felt like rain but colder and softer. My paws would get so cold it almost felt like they were burning. Sometimes, I walked on hard pebbles that really burned my paws. Mommy called it "rock salt" and said it was to melt the snow. She gently pulled me away from it and said, "Watch where you walk." After a few times of hearing her say this, I realized that I didn't have to walk on the rock salt. I could tip-toe around it. This helped a lot! We never walked for long in the winter. Mommy would get too cold because she didn't have fur. I got cold too, but Mommy and Sister put clothes on me. At first, I didn't like them. It felt awkward. As I got older, I decided that I did like them—most of them. I didn't like things on my head or ears. How could I hear everything? It made Mommy and Sister happy to see me in my outfits. The things I did for my humans! Winter was also the time for our Snow People, and it became the time we visited Brother. That was a good part of Winter!

Spring was wonderful. Everything was coming back to life. The trees started budding, there were a lot of baby animals, and the breeze carried a warmth behind it that promised sunshine and warmer days. There were two things I did not like about Spring. The first thing was rain. I didn't like to get my feet wet. I didn't like the feeling of rain hitting me while I relieved myself. I learned quickly how to run under the house awning so that I could relieve myself quickly with the least amount of rain hitting me. Sometimes we got caught by surprise on a walk, and Mommy had us run home. She wasn't as fast as me, but it was still fun to run in the rain. Mommy laughed and would dry me off with my special towel. She said we looked like sewer rats but was only joking.

The second thing about Spring that I didn't like was that Mommy sneezed all the time. The sneezing always startled me. I would run and hide under the table or bed whenever she sneezed. Sister sneezed too sometimes, but that didn't bother me. They sounded the same. I sneezed too. Mommy never ran from me when I sneezed. I wondered why Mommy's sneezing bothered me. I was weird.

The seasons came and went and repeated their patterns. It helped the animals know what to do and where to find shelter or protection. There were some seasons throughout my lifetime that had extreme weather. There was one time while living in the old apartment that a big storm came. The winds were so rough I nearly blew away even on my leash! Mommy said I looked like a little kite. I didn't know what that was, but I knew I didn't like the feeling of the wind lifting my feet off the ground. The apartment was cloaked in darkness during this storm. It was cold, and Mommy could not cook anything. We would snuggle under blankets all huddled together to stay warm. When we got exceptionally cold, we went inside the car, turned on the engine, and put the heat on. We stayed there for a little, listening to music and getting warm, but we didn't drive anywhere. The roads were completely covered in snow. The piles of snow were taller than Mommy that year. It was nice to feel the heat inside the car. Mommy was very clever. She always knew how to take care of things and us. I paid special attention during these moments. I wanted to be clever too.

Even though I didn't like snow, when the Sky stopped dropping snow and it settled into piles, I liked to run and climb on the piles. I would pretend I was Wolf, climbing and running on the icy mountain peaks. Wolf was a master at moving in the snow. He would look for food and run wild. It was so much fun pretending to be Wolf, remembering that I *was* Wolf. Then I would feel too cold and remembered that I did not have as much fur as Wolf, and Wolf's legs were longer. Sigh. I should have picked a bigger body.

There were other storms that were very rough. They usually occurred in Autumn or Winter. Winds were very strong and fierce. Many homes were destroyed by Nature.

Many animals were displaced or killed during these extreme storms. There is no match for Nature. She is Life and Death. Nature's rule is the only true rule. Animals know this. They respect natural law. They respect Universe and all its life forms. Animals only kill what they need and do not waste things. It is a cycle of life that keeps the world healthy. Humans do not understand this law. They think they are the true rulers. Nature tries to remind humans that they are wrong by sending these storms. It seems to me that Nature is sending more and more reminders to humans. I hope they listen. Bear agrees with me. We try to send our humans messages. Maybe they can help.

33

TIMES WERE CHANGING

I didn't know how to tell Mommy that things were about to change, and the change was going to be a big one.

Everything had been good here at home. Mommy was happy, and so was Sister. Sister worked a lot and went out with friends, so I didn't get to spend a lot of time with her; but when I did, it was so much fun. We took a lot of pictures, and she made me sit still for them. After a while, I knew when she was taking pictures. She didn't even have to tell me to sit still. I liked to look at her in the pictures. Sometimes, I would stare into the mirror at Sister sitting behind me. We were highly creative with our photo shoots.

I also started snuggling with Sister more when she was home. I would sneak out of Mommy's room and jump up on Sister's bed. She liked that. Mommy didn't even realize. I would go back inside before Mommy woke up and took my usual position on the bed. All these years, I could have snuggled with both Mommy and Sister. That thought made me laugh inside. I was a Silly Bear!

Mommy worked a lot too, but she always made time for me. She would come home in the middle of the day just to see me if her schedule at work allowed. I liked that. On those days, we would go for a quick walk so I could relieve myself. Then we sat and snuggled on the couch for a few minutes before she went back to work. I liked the little visits in the day, but I hated when she had to leave again.

How were things changing? I felt my body changing. I had to relieve myself more often. Mommy took me out five times a day. Sometimes I was able to walk for a very long time, but other times, I was just too tired. On those days, I only wanted to lie down. I continued to take my medicine in the morning with peanut butter, and I was eating well. Still, something was different.

We continued our small adventures to the park once a week when Mommy didn't have work. I knew we were going because she put all her clothes in a bag and carried it to the car. This meant we were doing chores and then the park. I always got excited when I saw the bag of clothes. Sometimes we stopped at a building and Mommy put money in a tube that traveled up and over to the lady behind a window. The lady always put a piece of paper back in the tube with a treat for me. Wow! I loved doing chores with Mommy! I didn't always eat the treat right away. If I didn't eat it, I would place it next to me to save it for when I was ready. I know other dogs would have eaten it right away. Not me. It is important to be frugal with your treats. You should never be gluttonous. You must be careful and sensible, even with treats. Plus, I was usually too excited to eat.

One of these chore days, we stopped off at the Vet. Sneaky Mommy! I didn't expect that. I wondered why I didn't see that in Mommy's mind. I was probably too excited about the park to really hear her thoughts. That's what happens. You can get distracted and not receive messages that may be important! I would try to be more attentive. Who knows what else I missed!

The girl at the Vet pricked me with a needle and made me relieve myself in a cup. How embarrassing! I hated to do that. At least Mommy didn't see that part of our visit. I didn't want her to see me in such an embarrassing situation. I sat in the big room with Mommy while we waited for the doctor. She walked from the back quickly. I didn't like her expression. Something was wrong. I felt Mommy's body tense up next to me. She knew something was wrong, too.

I knew it! The Vet said it was necessary for me to go on a special diet for my kidneys, plus take another medicine. I hated the special food for kidneys. Mommy had tried to give it to me after the last big sickness. It was disgusting. I didn't care what the Vet or Mommy said, I was not going to eat that. It tasted like a box. GROSS! Mommy was crying again. When she hugged me, it was harder than normal; it didn't hurt, it just felt different. She was upset. Really upset. She asked me again to stay with her forever.

"Don't ever leave me," she said. "Please! You are my baby, my best friend."

Oh, Mommy. I never want *to leave you.* For some reason, I could not promise her this time. Bear just nodded.

Mommy took me to the park as originally planned, and I forgot all about the food. We had fun at the park. There were ducks and an egret. The egret was a funny–looking bird. It had exceptionally long legs that looked like little twigs. It also had a very long beak. I smelled some pretty flowers, and a butterfly landed on my nose. This made Mommy laugh. I looked up at Mommy. We made a good team.

When I got back in the car, I noticed my treat from the window lady. I had almost forgotten about it. I sat in the back and munched on my treat. Delicious! Not like that gross box-tasting food I was going to have to eat. Ugh. I wished I didn't remember about the food. That just ruined my mood. Then I remembered what Bear said about living in the moment. I shook my body, making my necklace clink, then stood up and looked out the window. Mommy reached back to pet my head. She could barely reach me, so I leaned forward a little so she could reach my head. Then I ran back to the window to look at all the stores and people.

The new medicine was not bad. I didn't taste it mixed in the peanut butter. Mommy made me an egg in the morning and mixed it with the gross food. I ate the egg but spit out the food.

"Baby, you must eat your food! You need it to get better. You don't want to go back to the hospital, do you? Then we cannot be together," she said.

The hospital? Away from Mommy? Oh, boy! I sent Mommy a message. I asked her to please make the food taste better. Guess what? Mommy heard me. She came over and poured some vegetable liquid in and mixed it up.

She said, "Here you go, Sweetheart. Here's a nice stew."

I ate all the food. This made Mommy very happy. Honestly, I felt better having eaten. I did not realize how hungry I was until I ate the "stew."

Mommy spent a lot of time with me and was making sure I ate good things. I ate carrots, zucchini, egg whites, peanut butter, apples, and some other things. She said I was a good eater. I wanted Mommy to stop being afraid, so I ate the gross food even without the vegetable liquid. She also squirted some liquid in my mouth and called it medicine. I didn't like it. The taste was not too bad, but I didn't like that it had to be squirted in my mouth. I noticed, however, that since she started giving me that liquid medicine I was not in as much pain. I was able to move easier, and even slept better. It made Mommy happy to see me feeling better. All I wanted to do was make Mommy happy.

Life was like this now. Medicine, special foods, more walks. I also slept more. Sometimes, Mommy called me "old man." I knew she was teasing me, but I also knew there was a little truth in that.

We went to the Vet regularly; I was pricked and weighed each time. I stepped on the scale by myself when Mommy asked me. I knew to sit still while the girl looked at the top. Everyone was so impressed at my abilities. Pfft. They should have seen me jump the stone wall in our old neighborhood. That was impressive!

On one of the visits we got some great news. Everything was holding steady. I saw Mommy was greatly relieved. That made me happy. This moment felt important, but it could not be my purpose, could it? I mean, it was important to make Mommy happy, but that was just a small part of it, right? I decided to talk to Bear. Bear had all the answers. My real purpose would show itself soon, Bear said. I was excited, yet I was also nervous.

34

YOU ARE SO BEAUTIFUL

I was in Mommy's arms, and she was moving back and forth. We were dancing. Mommy sang softly in my ear along with the song playing on her friend Alexa, "You Are So Beautiful." I felt the energy around Mommy. It was bright and warm, glowing, and filled with love. I placed my paws on her shoulders and kissed her face. Mommy was so beautiful to me. I wished we could stay this way forever.

After dancing, we said goodbye to Alexa and sat on the couch to watch some TV. I didn't care what was on, so long as it wasn't anything too loud. I just enjoyed being close together. I was next to Mommy with my head on her lap. She was petting me and holding me close. Mommy put a thin blanket over us to keep us extra snuggly. Sister came home and saw us snuggling together. I looked up at her, wondering why anyone would disturb us at this time. My tail wagged. My tail showed that I was happy to see Sister. Sometimes I needed my tail to remind me to embrace happy moments.

Sister said, "You guys make me sick!" but she was laughing. This made Mommy laugh, which made my tail wag harder. I snuggled closer to Mommy and rested my head back down. I loved when we were all together. Before drifting off to sleep, I wondered about Brother. I wished he were here with us too. I missed him. Maybe we would visit him again. It did seem as if the weather was changing to cold. I would get to see Philip and Milo too. I fell asleep thinking about my pack, my family. I was very lucky, wasn't I? I was lucky to find my family. Lucky the box that held me and my littermates was found by the Rescuer. Lucky to have met Bear. No matter how scary life started, I made it through and met some important and special humans along the way. While thinking about all these things, I drifted to sleep.

I was often tired now. I felt more tired and tired more often. Sometimes I wanted to run around and play, but when I got up to do that, I just felt too tired. This made me sad. I lay down and rested my head on my paws. What was going on? I was eating the gross food. I was taking my medicine. I relieved myself often outside. I was doing everything Mommy said to do. Bear said that it was getting close to a special adventure I would take alone. That couldn't be true! I promised Mommy I would never leave her. I wanted to stay with her forever. Who would protect her? Who was going to take away all that negative energy that attached to her from work? Who would keep her company? Mommy needed me. I couldn't go on an adventure without her! We were a team. All our adventures were together. Plus, I wanted to stay. I wanted to see Sister and listen to her stories. I wanted to steal her socks only to return them unharmed. I wanted to find my purpose with my family.

Bear was always right, but he must be mistaken this time. Leave Mommy on an adventure by myself. Pffft! That was a ridiculous thought. I got angry, and I told Bear that he was wrong. I sat there in the hall and barked at him. He heard me. Mommy heard me too.

"What are you barking at, Baby? Are you losing your mind?" she asked me.

Sigh. Well, that was embarrassing. I didn't realize I barked out loud. I looked up at her and just walked to my water bowl for a drink. I'd try to play again tomorrow. Maybe I would feel better and have more energy tomorrow.

Bear never answered me. He wasn't mad at me. He was giving me space to think about things. Bear and Mommy were alike in some ways. Sometimes I wondered if they secretly spoke to one another.

ON THE ROAD AGAIN!

*I*t was getting cold, and we were getting out of here! We were going on another road trip to visit Brother. Bear was right. I was going on an adventure, but he was completely wrong about the circumstances. I couldn't wait to see everyone, even Milo. Sister bought us funny clothes to wear. So silly! I heard Mommy talking to Brother. She was telling him about my last sickness. I wasn't feeling well, and my kidneys were getting worse. She said the medication and diet seemed to be helping but that I just had to relieve myself a lot. That was embarrassing. I hoped Brother didn't think me a baby.

We did our usual trip filled with stops and the hotel room. I was so excited to get to Brother's house. The traveling was not too bad, but it was good to finally arrive. Brother had something on his foot. It was some type of cast. Mommy seemed worried about it. He was also using these big sticks under his arms to help him walk around. We were all told to be careful around Brother so as not to bump his foot because it hurt a lot. I understood what that meant. Maybe Mommy should give him some of my medicine. It seemed to help me sometimes.

I got along well with Philip and Milo. We played together and ran around outside. I got tired quickly, so I didn't play as much as I wanted. Milo was not as annoying as he was last year. I guess we were all getting older. The three of us followed Mommy around. She talked to us and petted us and paid a lot of attention to us. When all the humans went out, the three of us stayed home together. I was not afraid this year. I knew Mommy would come back; the company was nice too. We were all well–behaved. Except Milo peed a little on the floor. Philip and I pretended it didn't happen. Mommy saw it when they got home and cleaned it up right away. She didn't tell Brother or Courtney, Milo's human. Courtney and Milo had been living with Brother for a few years now. They had a nice pack. Brother, Courtney, Philip, Milo, and Frank, a snake! Mommy whispered to Milo that he shouldn't pee on the floor. I think Milo heard her. He was good the rest of the time, either going outside or using the pads left out for him.

Something was weird about this trip, though. Everyone seemed a little grumpy. The only time everyone was happy was when they played with me, Philip, and Milo. I understood Brother didn't feel well. He was in pain and couldn't move around too well. Everyone else had no excuse. I would never understand humans. Such complicated beings.

Mommy said this was probably our last visit for a while. Everyone asked why. She said that things were changing, and everyone had jobs to worry about. She said it would be hard to plan a time that worked for everyone. Then Mommy looked at me, and she almost started crying. I turned my head away from her. I did not want her to see what I was thinking. I had been thinking about the adventure Bear told me I would be going on alone. I realized now that he meant my time here was coming to an end.

Mommy knew it was close to my time, too. She didn't want to talk about it, but I heard her thoughts. She didn't want it to be true. She was scared. I wanted to find a way to get better, but I didn't think there was one! Sister changed the subject and we pushed these thoughts away. Bear always visited me. He was always with me, even if he didn't say anything.

I heard Bear whisper "Be strong, Little One. It's your purpose."

My purpose. My purpose? I was getting tired of hearing about my purpose. Why couldn't my purpose just present itself? Why did I have to wait and wonder? Was I supposed to choose my purpose, or did my purpose choose me? Being an adult was hard, even for me—a dog. Decisions, sickness, patience, understanding. . . all these things were not part of puppyhood. Well, my puppyhood wasn't that easy. But it wasn't as hard as being a grown–up dog either! Sigh.

The ride back home was a lot of fun. Mommy and sister were extra silly! They were singing and laughing and gave me little treats in the back seat. The more they laughed, the higher our moods rose. Seems that laughter really is the best medicine. The trucks didn't scare me quite so much anymore. I still didn't like them, but I didn't feel the need to crouch down and hide from them either. Mommy called me brave. She said this with a big smile, and I could see how proud she was of me. That reminded me of Diesel's comment about me being a soldier and warrior. Yes! I was brave! I *am* brave! I closed my eyes and dreamt of Wolf. And Athena. Beautiful Athena, Mommy's dog from years ago, who crossed over the Bridge . . .

36

ATHENA, ROXIE, AND THE OTHERS

*W*inter was very cold that year. We didn't have a lot of snow, but when we did it was high. The part that was hardest to deal with was the temperature. I had never felt this cold in my life. Mommy tried to put boots on my feet to help me with the snow and salt, but I didn't like them and flipped them off my feet. Mommy put her boots on without a problem. It took a long time to get ready for a walk. Mommy put on so many things before she would go outside. Then once we were outside, I was so cold and tired that we barely walked at all! I was the one to drag Mommy back to the house. She would walk more if I asked her. Maybe. She hated the cold too.

Mommy had been practicing Animal-Speak and had even managed to talk to animals we didn't know. She spoke to a horse named Finn, a few dogs, an elephant, and most important to this story, her dogs from years ago, Athena and Roxie. Athena and Roxie live where Wolf lives now, in Joy. Mommy said they crossed the Rainbow Bridge. Roxie was a Rottweiler; she was still lingering around the base of the bridge. She was sad and tormented. She wouldn't move forward into Joy. Athena was a Springer Spaniel and she visited the base of the Bridge to talk to Mommy. There was a mixture of happiness and sadness when

Mommy talked to Athena. I heard their conversations. I didn't say anything because that would be rude. But I could hear them.

At first, it was with great excitement for Mommy that Athena came forward. She showed Mommy that she was mastering Animal-Speak; she also showed her that life after Life was real and beautiful. The more Mommy spoke to Athena, the sadder she became. It wasn't sadness about Athena; it was sadness because she realized Athena's purpose for visiting.

Athena was a very nurturing dog in her other life with Mommy. She helped her care for little kittens and was able to see spirits that lingered in one of their apartments. It was with great sadness that Mommy had to give Athena to another human. She could not care for her properly. It nearly broke her heart, but she had Brother and was pregnant with Sister at the time, and Mommy's life was falling apart. She was left alone and had to figure everything out on by herself. Mommy felt awful and sometimes still cried about it. Athena assured her that she knew Mommy's heart, and she had been happy with her new human. He had a farm and plenty of room to run and play. He took excellent care of her until her time came. That helped Mommy a little, but she was still sad. Athena was fulfilling her life's purpose in the Life after Life. She was called a Greeter. Athena's job was to help others cross the Rainbow Bridge and show them the way to go. There were many Greeters. They usually hung out some-where else, until they received a call from either a human or an animal needing help to cross over.

Mommy was smart. She realized that Athena showing up so much meant she was getting ready to help someone cross over. . . to help *me* cross over. I could see Athena and some others, and I turned my back to them. No! I was going to get better. Mommy needed me here! I would *Never* leave her! *Never!* Mommy looked at me. Her eyes were scared yet so full of love.

Don't worry Mommy, I won't leave you!

There were crows outside. More crows than I can remember this time of year. They kept landing on the tree in front of the deck. They faced the deck and cawed loudly. I barked at them to shut up. They cawed, I barked. Mommy laughed.

"What are you guys saying?" she asked.

I quietly said, "You don't want to know, Mommy."

I hated those crows. I wished they would mind their own business. I barked loudly at them and walked inside.

I watched Mommy carefully. More than I usually did. She never took time to rest. She was always doing something. The only time she rested was when I lay on top of her. So, I did that a lot. Plus, I got to hear her heartbeat and feel her breath moving up and down. It was comforting to me. We comforted each other. Funny how that works.

I did something out of love for Mommy, and I got love in return.

I began seeing shadows of things crossing the room. I followed them with my eyes. What were they? What did they want? Why were they here? I gave my low, threatening growl.

Mommy looked at me and said, "Do you see something, Baby?"

I believe she saw them too. *Don't worry. I am Wolf. I will get rid of these shadows AND those stupid crows!*

I closed my eyes and felt Mommy petting me, slow and gentle. She whispered she loved me, and I fell asleep. I dreamt of Wolf again. Wolf was racing through the woods with his humans. He was faster and had to stop often for them to catch up. I could feel the wind blowing. The Sun was warm and bright. These woods were different than any I remembered. There was no danger in them. It was beautiful. The deer were not scared of Wolf. They ran alongside him without a care in the world.

The humans were laughing, holding hands, and skipping. They stopped to smell flowers and drink from the stream. Wolf drank too. The water was cool and clear and delicious. On the other side of the stream, there were other animals. All different kinds. They also were not afraid of Wolf. Everyone lived together peacefully. It was a most amazing place. I didn't want to leave. I heard a sound in the distance. A siren. Wolf stopped dead in his tracks and threw his head back releasing a long, loud howl.

Suddenly, Mommy and Sister came to me. I was back in my room on the bed. I was howling. This made them laugh. I looked at them, slightly confused. I was in the woods, but I was here. I was Wolf, but I was me. Life was funny. Life after Life was beautiful. Maybe Mommy and Sister could come with me on the next adventure. Maybe I didn't have to go alone. They would love it.

"Bear," I called to him. "I understand I will be going on an adventure. Can Mommy and Sister come too?"

I knew the answer before Bear responded. I was not a young soul like Philip. I had been on similar journeys before. I was an old soul. I knew we didn't get to pick the time, place, or company for our final journey. I knew this. I asked anyway, wishfully.

"No, Little One. But you know this. They have more work to do in this Life. You have work to do in the next one. Remember your purpose? It will all become clear soon," Bear said.

I was so tired of hearing about my purpose. Why was it taking so long to show itself? What if my purpose was simply to be Mommy's best friend? Wasn't that enough? I was getting frustrated. I wanted to bite something. I ran in Sister's room and went through her laundry bag and grabbed whatever I could get my teeth on. I dragged her clothes under the bed. I ripped them and tore a big hole in them. I heard the door and could tell it was Mommy. I came out from under the bed and greeted her at the stairs. I loved saying hello to Mommy after a long day. She hugged me and we went for a walk. I was feeling better. Maybe all I needed was to rip Sister's clothes.

I AM TEN YEARS OLD!

There was excitement in the air! Mommy and Sister came in the bedroom and snuggled me and kissed me a thousand times. They said, "Happy Birthday, Baby!" and told me I was ten years old. I didn't really know what that meant, but I knew it was special. They both left for the day and promised to celebrate when they returned. Celebrate! Wow! All because of me! I felt special and important. I remembered celebrations for Sister and Mommy's birthdays. I also remembered past celebrations for me; yet, somehow this one seemed more important. I was excited and could not wait for their return.

I spent the day in my usual way. I drank, ate a little bit, did several patrol walks around the apartment, thought about taking a sock from Sister's room but changed my mind, and jumped up on the bed to nap and look out the window. I barked at the Mailman when I saw him walking toward the house. He looked up and waved his hand at me. That made me laugh inside. I saw Lexi in the neighbor's yard, and we talked a little bit. She was my girlfriend.

I had helped Mommy get Lexi back to her home one day when she got loose and ran across the street. We ran outside and called to her. Then Mommy decided to go across the street so

Lexi wouldn't run in front of a car. Lexi almost ran from Mommy until she saw me. I told her to come with me, and she did. She liked me. A lot. It was at that moment that she became my special girlfriend. We touched noses and licked each other. She promised to always be my special girlfriend, and I promised her too. Sometimes I wanted to get close to her and I would whine loudly so she could hear me. She would look up at the deck barking and made cute little noises in response. Other times, I heard her barking at her humans. She wanted to go in the house. She would bark and bark, then run to the fence and bark up to me on the deck. I barked loudly so her humans would hear. They did. They let her back in the house. Another job well done on my part. I felt proud. Lexi knew I liked her, but we were confined by our humans and our positions. We made the most of the situation. We talked to each other all the time. We understood each other.

We pets are not totally free. We appreciate our lives with humans and really do love our families, but sometimes the idea of being totally free is overwhelming. We all want freedom. Freedom from restraints. Freedom from restrictions. Humans do too, I suppose. I know Mommy dreamt of freedom. At least we have each other in this not–so–free life.

When Mommy and Sister came home, they were all teeth. They were extremely excited about my birthday. I didn't really feel well by the end of the day, but I wagged my tail and acted excited too. That made them happy. There were presents and a cake just for me. Mommy and Sister sang the "Happy Birthday" song to me. I wanted to hide under the table. Mommy was *not* a good singer. I didn't hide though. That would have been rude on such a special day. The cake was delicious. I was only allowed a few pieces because of my illness. I savored every bite. It tasted like pumpkin and apples. I would have more tomorrow. I licked my lips at the thought.

Next it was time to open my presents. I loved to rip off the paper that hid the surprise inside. That was fun. I got a new

Lambchop snuggly, some special treats, and a bone. I grabbed my new snuggly and brought it immediately into the bedroom. Then I came back in the living room and looked up at the table to make sure my cake was still there. All was good.

So I was ten! I felt like this was a turning point in my life. I was a real grownup now. I decided that I should try to overcome my fears, like trucks, rain, loud noises, and the Avenue. I *was* doing better with trucks, at least when we were in the car. I didn't want to think about that anymore. For now, I was enjoying my special day with my family. I jumped up on the couch right between Mommy and Sister so they could both pet me. I loved spending snuggle time with them.

Sister took a lot of pictures of me, me with Sister, me with Mommy. She enjoyed taking pictures. To be honest, I was very photogenic. I looked at the pictures on her phone as she showed Mommy. Some of them were very funny. Sister added silly pictures on top of the photograph. One picture of me had a little birthday hat to commemorate the day! We had a lot of fun together. This was a most excellent birthday.

Bear wished me a happy day too, of course. He never forgot about me. Besides Mommy and Sister, Bear was my closest friend. More than a friend, really. We were bonded together, and I loved him. Today was a great day.

38

FOOD, GLORIOUS FOOD

I loved food, especially the food Mommy cooked. She liked to give me tastes of things while she cooked. Sometimes she dropped food on the floor as she was chopping vegetables, and I would run to grab it and gobble it up. Mommy laughed. I had learned to stay close but not too close. I remembered when I was little and got bopped in the face with her feet because I was too close. It didn't hurt, but it was uncomfortable. I also had my paws stepped on a few times. I squealed in pain. The worst part of that was that Mommy felt horrible about it. So, I learned to keep a few steps back so as not to cause any incidents.

I also liked to watch, as you must have figured out by now. I noticed that Mommy moved from one part of the kitchen to the stove and then stood there stirring things and watching things cook. The longer things cooked, the more the kitchen was filled with delicious smells of the food. When she was not looking, I stood in front of the stove on my back legs and leaned on the handle of the oven with my front paws. I was pretending to cook and hoping to grab something. I heard Mommy laugh in her head and say, "Silly Bear! Be careful you don't get burned." I guess she did see me. Mommy saw everything, even when her eyes were not directly on me.

Food was a big part of our lives. It was not just for sustenance; it was for celebrations, time spent together, and enjoyment. Mealtime was a time when Mommy and Sister stopped running around and sat down together to share food. I liked mealtime. Everyone slowed down. I sat watching them eat. I knew I would get some when they were finished. It was always delicious.

I got in the habit of eating my food late at night. There was a reason for this. I waited for everyone to be settled in bed safely. Then I could eat my food and get fuel for my night watch; also, eating late gave me a full belly to help me sleep better through the night in between my patrols. It was a good routine. I made it up myself. Mommy always left food out for me, but I did not eat it mindlessly. I ate when I was hungry. My big meal was at night, and I nibbled during the day.

I wasn't feeling very hungry since my birthday. Nothing felt right in my stomach. This worried Mommy.

"You are a skinny Little Bear! You have to eat," she said.

I just couldn't. Mommy said it was three days since she filled my bowl, and the bowl was still full. This was not good, and I could tell it upset her. Mommy decided to start cooking my food from scratch, like she did with her meals. No more of the dry kibble. She made some rice, quinoa, veggies, and chicken. It was delicious! I gobbled up my meal so fast. This made Mommy happy. I walked over to her to thank her, and when Mommy leaned over for a kiss I burped in her face. Mommy laughed. She said I was rude, but she was joking. She liked when I ate. I felt better with this food, too. I was a warrior after all. I needed my strength. I was going to get better! I *must*.

I ate well for a while. Everything seemed better. I was not in so much pain. I had more energy for walks. I even began walking on the Avenue! I followed Coqui's scent. Coqui liked to walk on the Avenue. It wasn't so scary when I focused on Coqui's scent instead of where I was walking. I stopped often to look up and then kept walking. Mommy was so impressed with me and said I was very brave. Of course I was. I was ten, after all. Not a baby. I really did feel great. My poops were better too, according to Mommy. She analyzed everything, as embarrassing as that was. Even my breath was better for a while.

This burst of health did not last very long. I kept trying to eat but nothing felt right in my stomach again. I did my best. I ate what I could, yet I felt myself getting skinnier. My fur was also drier, not as soft as normal. My mouth tasted bad; Mommy's nose scrunched up when I breathed in her face. I felt the worry on Mommy. I felt her eyes watching everything I did. She noticed my leg dragging slightly. She noticed my eyes were not as bright and sharp. Mommy noticed I was slowing down in my walks too. I needed to rest so I could fight this and get better. I was so tired. I was not sure how to get better. I was not sure I *would* get better.

Sometimes, I could not even make it up the stairs and Mommy had to carry me. I no longer felt embarrassed by this. I appreciated her help. Sister helped me too. That is what we do for family, right? We help each other. Nothing to be embarrassed about.

39

UNDERSTANDING

Sister went into the hospital. Mommy took her in the morning and then came back with her. She looked tired and hurt. I didn't know what happened. Mommy was paying a lot of attention to her. She gave her massages and fed her in her room. She helped her get up and fixed her bed. I didn't mind. I loved Sister. It's just that Mommy looked so tired. She was working, taking care of Sister, and taking care of me. No one was taking care of Mommy. I went in Sister's room and rested with her. We were both so tired. Maybe if we rested together Mommy would be able to get some rest too.

Sister teased Mommy. "Little Bear is with *me*," she called out.

Mommy laughed. "Whatever!" she said jokingly.

They liked to play fight over me. I was *that* special.

I heard Bear speaking. "It's time, Little One."

No. Bear, it is not time. I couldn't leave them now. Everything was a mess. They needed me to be here. I was not ready. They were not ready. This was not the time. I lifted my head up anxiously. *Why would Bear say this to me?* Everyone needed to get back on track. Sister needed to heal. I needed to get better. Mommy needed to rest. This was not the time!

The crows were assembled outside on the tree. They cawed loudly. I was too tired to answer them. I saw Athena more often too. She sat patiently at the end of the Bridge. Sometimes, I started to walk on the Bridge. I always stopped in the middle, though. I looked at Athena, then back at the front end where Mommy and Sister lived with all the things that were familiar. I never moved closer to Athena. I would turn and slowly walked back. It was not time. Not just yet.

Mommy was doing very well with Animal-Speak. She talked to me all the time. I knew she heard me too. We would talk to each other while she was away at work. I liked that. It kept me company while I rested on the bed. I liked to listen to her talking to the other animals, too. She talked a lot with Athena.

Talking to Roxie was a big development. Roxie had a lot of guilt and sadness over her puppies. She did not have a happy life when she went to live with her first owner. He took Roxie away from Mommy when Brother was born. He was not a good human. He kept her chained and alone and made her have babies. When the babies were born, Roxie killed them. She wanted to save them from a bad life. Her bad human killed her because of it; he lost money he would have made from selling her puppies. Mommy spoke gently to Roxie. She showed Roxie love. Mommy helped Roxie find her babies on the other side of the Bridge. Once she saw the babies, she moved away from the Bridge and entered the place called Joy. She stayed with her puppies all the time and played with them. Mommy helped Roxie fully transition and live her life after Life happily; this was possible because I helped her remember Animal-Speak. I was proud of this. I was immensely proud of Mommy.

Sister was getting better. She went back to work. Mommy still had not rested. I needed to go out a lot to relieve myself. I stood at the top of the stairs when it was time to go. I looked down the stairs. Then I looked up at Mommy.

"Okay, Little One. I'll carry you. My little Baby Bear!"

She kissed my head when she picked me up. Mommy was cloaked in fear. We got outside, and I walked slowly. I looked in each direction to decide which way I wanted to go. I wanted to see my friends, but I didn't have the energy. I turned in the other direction and walked where Coqui walked, following her scent. We just walked one block and then I lay on the cool grass. It felt so good. I rolled onto my back, and Mommy laughed. Hearing Mommy laugh made me realize that Mommy did not laugh much lately. This made me sad.

Mommy and I were outside. We saw the Mailman. I decided to make peace with him. It was time. I walked over to him and sat down right at his feet. He seemed surprised. Mommy was chatting with him, and he seemed really pleased that I was letting him pet me. He was not a bad guy after all. I felt silly for yelling at him for so many years. So much time wasted, as Bear would say.

We continued our walk. I was hoping to see my human friend AJ. He was an old soul. We were friends in another life and somehow found each other here. I recognized him immediately, and he was also so happy to see me. Whenever he was outside, he called out to me, and I pulled on the leash so I could reach him fast to say hello. On this walk, we saw AJ briefly. He was standing behind a fence. He said hello but could not pet me through the fence. He understood my situation; he looked sad. I looked at him and without making a sound, we understood each other. I loved seeing friends, old and new. I saw a few other friends on the walk. I went nose to nose with them. They understood what was happening with me as well. We said goodbye.

The next few days were blurry to me. Sometimes Mommy had to carry me home because I was unable to continue. She held me tight to her chest. I felt her heartbeat. Mommy never complained. I knew she loved me. I was so lucky to have found my human so quickly this lifetime. I remembered my days as Wolf with my human. She was kind and sweet and caring.

Mommy had not changed over time. She was the same. Not totally the same. She was sadder in this Life. Sad and fearful. Life had thrown many things at her, things that hurt her deeply. Poor Mommy.

The only time that Mommy was genuinely happy was when she was with me and my skin-siblings. Then Mommy glowed. Wasn't there someone who could love Mommy the way I did? Someone who would protect her? Someone to keep her company and make her laugh? Hm.

"Bear!" I called to him. "Why am I thinking like this? Why do I want Mommy to find another human?"

Bear answered me, "Because, Little One, you want her to be happy. The greatest show of love is wanting someone to be loved and happy even if that is without you."

Without me. Yes, she would be without me. I understood that now.

My physical body was failing. We all knew this. I could not fight it anymore. I tried because I didn't want to leave my family. I tried because I knew my family did not want me to leave. It went both ways. Our love was mutual and strong. I should have had more time in this physical body. I was only ten years old. There was more I wanted to see, more I wanted to do. Mainly, I just wanted to remain with my humans forever. That was not how Life worked, however. The physical body could only handle so much. I was a little scared. Scared for me, scared for my humans. Yet, I knew that I would always be with them. Maybe I knew this because I had other lives. Maybe it was because Athena and Bear helped me to understand. Whatever the reason, I knew. Knowing this made it less scary.

Knowing that Mommy fully embraced Animal-Speak was a big help. I knew we would be able to talk together even after I crossed the Rainbow Bridge. I knew this, and it brought me comfort. But still. . .

There was nothing to pack where I was going. Nothing to bring with me. I knew there were many wonderful Souls waiting for me, and in turn, I would be there waiting for others when their time came. I thought of Mommy's favorite song, "Bye Bye Blackbird." Music is wonderful. It can make you happy, sad, or just give comfort. Right now, I was feeling a little of everything.

I'll be waiting for you, Mommy. You too, Sister and Brother. I will be waiting for you always.

40

GOODBYE, MY LOVE

I could not eat anymore. I did not even want to drink. But I did suddenly have a craving for turkey slices. Mommy was at work, so I sent her a message. I asked her to bring home turkey slices. I hoped she heard me. All I wanted was turkey slices like when I was in the hospital. Mommy came home with some grocery bags. I perked up and got excited. Did she get it? Yes! Mommy heard me! Yay! Oh, how I loved turkey slices. These were delicious. I ate about five slices. Mommy told me to save some for later. I could hardly wait for later. We went out for a walk. Not much of one. I was tired. Mommy carried me upstairs, giving me kisses on my head.

We snuggled together at night. I slept much deeper now. Mommy had her arm around me like she had started doing and held my paw like she did when I was that tiny puppy in the crate on those first nights together. I loved to sleep like this. I heard her heartbeat. The rhythm of her heart helped me sleep.

I woke up in the middle of the night. I felt sick. I thumped off the bed and walked toward the stairs. I threw up all the turkey slices. I did it quietly. No one heard me. They would find it later. I went back to bed and stayed close to Mommy. I woke up early because my stomach was churning. I threw up again, this time I didn't make it off the bed. Mommy heard me this time.

"Oh, no! Baby, what's wrong?" Mommy said.

She cleaned it up right away and got dressed quickly. Mommy carried me down the stairs and saw my throw up from the middle of the night. I looked up at her face with sorrow in my eyes. She was not angry. She understood. We came back from a little walk and I just wanted to go back to bed. I jumped to get up on the bed and almost missed the top. I remembered when I was able to jump five feet in the air, literally. That was a long time ago. On the walk we used to pass a house with a high stone wall in front; I was able to leap up to the top without a problem. *Did I mention that already?* My memory was failing just like my athletic skills.

I was lying on the bed. It hurt to breathe. My leg twitched from pain or just from my insides failing. I didn't know which. Maybe both. Mommy was crying. She lay down next to me. She was whispering to me. She was whispering and petting me. Mommy was telling me how much she loved me. She was saying that I was her best friend and that I helped her in so many ways. She said she understood that it was time for me to live with Athena and the Others. She said it was okay and not to worry about her or Sister. All this was being whispered to me while she was crying. Mommy's voice was in my head as I drifted off. Athena was coming forward. I started walking and found myself back on the Bridge. Athena was there waiting for me. All I had to do was walk across the Bridge toward Athena and I would be out of pain. My suffering would end. I walked slowly. I stopped suddenly and turned to the front end.

"Mommy! Come with me! It looks so beautiful here," I called out.

Athena told me it was not her time. She was being patient with me. I took another step forward. Then I stopped again. I heard Sister. She just came home. I ran back to the front of the bridge and woke up. I didn't want to leave them. I wanted to stay. Or I wanted them to come with me. I called out to Bear.

"Tell me what to do, Bear. Tell me how I can change what is happening. I love them so much. Tell me what to do!"

Bear answered me. "It will be what it will be, Little One. Trust in yourself. All will be fine."

Mommy and Sister brought me back to the Vet. They pricked me, and we waited in the big room. There were other dogs in main room, a puppy and a few older ones. They asked me why I was there. I told them it was my time, but my humans didn't believe it to be true. They were sad for me. They came over and licked my face. The puppy didn't understand. He was very cute, so curious and new. I remembered being little, with my best friend and littermates. That seemed so long ago. I remembered being a little wolf cub. That was even longer ago. I remembered all the other lives I had lived. All those lives that led me to this moment in this Life. I should know my purpose by now, shouldn't I? What *was* my purpose?

I sat down quietly on the bench to think while we waited for the doctor to call us in.

I saw Athena in my mind. She was wagging her tail and calling to me. Mommy heard her too.

"No, Athena! Not just yet. Please," Mommy said.

I kissed her.

"Thank you, stinky breath!" she said in return and kissed me back.

Sister stayed with us for the entire visit. I'd heard Mommy talking to her earlier. She didn't want to take me alone. I didn't blame her. They would need each other now.

As suspected, the news was horrible. My body was failing me. That explained why I had stinky breath along with all the other ailments. Mommy was crying. Sister was crying on the inside. I could feel her pain. The doctor said we could try a few things, like staying in the hospital, needles, and more medicine. I hoped Mommy said no. It was too much, and it would not make a difference. Mommy asked the doctor if she thought it would help me; she asked if I would get better if we did those things.

The doctor put her eyes down and said, "Maybe for a few weeks."

A few more weeks. That was it. Except it would be a few more weeks in the hospital away from Mommy and Sister. I wished I could speak human so I could shout out my thoughts to the doctor and my family. *Shouldn't I have a say in this? Shouldn't I be able to decide my own fate?* I exhaled slowly. Mommy heard me and nodded her head. She asked the doctor if we could leave for a bit and come back later. I knew what that meant. I felt a little scared. I was also relieved.

Mommy and Sister took me for a ride. They had a plan for us, our last day together. We went to get a cheeseburger and ice cream, just for me. We took the food to my favorite park so we could have a little picnic. I wished I had strength to walk the trails, but I was so very tired.

I led Mommy toward the pond. I liked the pond. That would be good enough; that would be perfect. We walked slowly. I walked close to the pond so I could smell the water and the plants that grew there. I saw a turtle sitting on a log. The ducks were sitting in the water, not swimming but resting. The egret was in the middle of the pond standing tall on one leg, the other leg tucked under his wing. Funny way to stand, I thought.

Then we sat on a bench that was almost halfway around the pond. Mommy and Sister gave me some of the cheese-burger. It was delicious. I could not eat a lot, but I did have a good amount. Next came the ice cream. That was delicious too. This was real ice cream, not the dog version of ice cream. I lapped up right from the cup and got ice cream on my face and nose! This made them laugh. I looked at them and did it again. Then I drank water from Mommy's water bottle. I did not even spill a drop. The rest of the burger and ice cream were thrown into the garbage. I was not hungry. I ate more for the ceremony of the moment, for the flavors, and mainly to allow my humans to feel good about this moment. Mommy and Sister wanted to do something special with me because they loved me. I knew that. Although I was ready to meet Athena, I knew this was an important step for them. For me too.

We walked together a little more. I made some new friends on the path. I had a little more energy from the burger, so my tail wagged, and I held my head up high. You must always present yourself in the best way possible. These new friends wanted to know if I would be back again. I told them I would not. The older dogs understood; the younger ones were uncertain. I had wanted to see my usual friends, but they were not out today. I peed on a few trees and left my scent so they would know I was there. I asked the new friends to say goodbye to the others if they ever met them. They said they would. We kissed, and I looked up at Mommy. She was smiling, sort of.

Sister took a lot of pictures of me near the flowers. I leaned up on the stones and put my face close to them. I was posing. She said I looked like a model. I was quite handsome, even with all the gray hair that covered half of my face. I was distinguished, Mommy said. A butterfly flew close to my head. I watched it fluttering around me. Springtime. I liked Spring, except for all the rain. I guess I was leaving at a good time; I would not have to deal with the rain.

We drove back home for a little while. There was a strange feeling lingering in the air. The energy was heavy, expectant. I briefly walked around the apartment to survey the area. I was still on duty, after all. I took my job seriously. After a quick surveillance, we hung out together in the living room. They kept watching me. They didn't talk much. When they did, their words seemed hard to come through their heavy, tight breath. Mommy picked me up and we danced. I can't remember if there was music on this time, but Mommy was humming. Her heartbeat was not steady. I put my paws on her shoulders and leaned into her neck with my head. I loved dancing. Mommy held me tighter.

After the dance, I sat on the floor, positioned so I could see both Mommy and Sister. Remember, positioning is everything. Sister sat on the floor with me and petted me. She was extremely nervous. She was not sure what to say or do. I understood her. She wanted this to go away. I did too. We *all* did.

Time passed, and we were still at home. I was ready. I didn't feel well. It was my time. Athena was standing at the foot of the Bridge now. I knew she would greet me, and I was ready to meet her. Mommy and Sister were stalling. I understood why. I didn't want to leave them either. I got up and walked to the deck. It was quiet outside. The crows were there, many of them, but they were silent.

"Creepy crows," I heard Mommy say.

I sat there, uneasy on my feet. My head felt heavy; it was hard to hold it up. Mommy saw me, noticing my head bobbing.

"Baby! What are you doing?" she asked me. I turned my head and looked at her, unable to move my physical body.

I was walking across the Bridge.

Mommy carried me inside. It was time to go. They didn't want to take me back, but they understood. Hanging around was just postponing what needed to be done. We went downstairs, and I saw Coqui. I gave her a quick kiss. The landlord was outside too. He petted me and we said goodbye. I thought I saw his mouth quiver; he was crying inside. Mommy opened the car door for me, but instead of going in the back, *my* backseat, I jumped in the front onto sister's lap. She needed me close now. I needed her close, too.

It was different up front. I was able to see things as Mommy saw them. This was exciting. My last little adventure! Mommy reached out and held my paw. She said she was sorry she could not heal me. She was sorry she couldn't do more. *Oh, Mommy. You did everything. You were everything to me!*

At the Vet's again. This time we went straight back into a

new room. It looked pretty. I was too tired to patrol the area, but I scanned the room with my eyes. There was a big couch, a few chairs, and a fireplace. There were nice pictures of dogs on the wall and some other decorative pieces. It looked like a living room. We sat on the couch close together. Mommy and Sister took off my leash and harness and then took off my necklace. They were placed on the couch next to us. I glanced down at my necklace, at first worried that I was not wearing it. Then I remembered. I did not need it where I was going.

I sat on Mommy's lap and looked at Sister. Sister, with her beautiful face and loving eyes. I could stare at her forever. The doctor came in to put one last prick in my leg. Then I settled on Mommy's lap while she petted me, looking at Sister the whole time. A picture of Brother flashed before me. I wished I had seen him again to say goodbye. He was a great Brother. I loved him, too. I learned so much from watching him.

I suddenly felt sleepy and started drifting asleep. I knew this was hard on them, but they stayed with me the entire time. The love they showed me to the very end meant so much to me. They were my family. Our souls would forever be together.

I heard Mommy say, "Goodbye, my Love! Please visit me often."

I will! I love you. I love you both.

41

DRIFTING

I felt myself floating through the air. It was dark, but not scary. I drifted up and felt my body get lighter and lighter. My body didn't hurt anymore. I opened my eyes and looked around. I didn't see anything yet. I looked down and saw Mommy. She was holding my body. She was crying so hard. Sister was crying too. Wait! Could I change my mind? I wanted to be with them. My place is next to them to comfort them.

"See how they are crying? See how their hearts hurt so much? I must go to them and ease their pain!" I called out to Spirit. I kept drifting upwards. Nothing I thought was changing the direction. "No! I made a mistake. Please! Let me go back to them!" I called out again. I closed my eyes wishing to reverse the direction. I kept drifting north.

There was a ray of light creeping into the darkness. It was bright but didn't hurt my eyes. I followed the light, and I saw something in the distance. The Bridge. I stopped floating and landed at one end of the bridge. Athena was at the other end. She was standing up, wagging her tail, and barking some welcoming barks.

"Come on, Little Bear! It's okay. We have been waiting for you."

I took a few steps toward her. I could still hear Mommy and Sister crying behind me. I didn't want to keep walking. I held my position at the front of the Bridge. Frozen. Hesitant. What I must do and what I wanted to do were two different things. I knew from my life as Wolf that I really didn't have a choice but to cross the Bridge. Yet I was still drawn to Mommy and Sister.

"Can I just sit here for a little while, Athena? Please," I asked her.

She sat down and barked. She would wait there for me. She understood I needed time to adjust. I sat down and positioned myself so that I could see both ends of the Bridge with just a turn of my head. I was not afraid. It was not fear that kept me sitting at the base of the Bridge. It was love. To be completely honest, it was also the fact that I was not sure if I had properly fulfilled my purpose. I decided to take some time to reflect on my life as Little Bear. I lay down and looked toward Mommy and Sister. So much pain and sadness were surrounding them. I wondered if Mommy would hear me if I spoke to her. I would try.

"Mommy!" I called out to her.

I saw Mommy take a sudden breath. "Oh, Baby! I still feel you here. Please come back! Please! I don't want to be without you here!" and she cried harder.

Mommy and Sister were back in the car. They were driving home. I saw them walking slowly toward the steps. Coqui was barking at them. She never barked at them. I understood what she was saying. She was asking where I was. This made Mommy cry harder. I would have to send Coqui a message, so she understood. Even though we said goodbye, Coqui was a young soul. She didn't have a full understanding of how Life worked. My humans walked upstairs to our apartment. Mommy was standing there, staring at my things. She walked slowly through each room. She cried harder.

"I'm here, Mommy! Lie down on the bed. Rest with me a bit," I told her.

Mommy lay down sobbing, holding my elephant and the blanket she made for me. I was still lying on the Bridge, but I was able to send my energy and love to her. I focused my energy into a ball and laid it down next to her belly. She cried herself to sleep. Sister was on her bed, buried under the covers.

My purpose. What was my purpose? Did I fulfill it? I called out to Bear.

"Bear! Can you still hear me?" I asked.

"Yes, Little One. We will always be connected through time and space. Did you have a comfortable journey?"

"It was okay, I guess. Mommy and Sister were there so I was not afraid. I am watching them from the base of the Bridge. I want to go home to comfort them but know I can't. I feel stuck. I also wanted to know if you think I fulfilled my purpose," I said to him. Bear chuckled.

"Review your life with these humans, Little One. Think about it from before you entered the body of you as a puppy. What do *you* think?"

I thought about everything. I saw my life flash before me as if it were on the TV, every detail, every moment. I saw the joy I brought to my humans, but I also saw the transitions Mommy made because of me. I gave her peaceful nights, a sense of security, a reason to not run away; I gave Mommy a routine that helped her stay grounded, gave her comfort and company when she was alone; I helped Mommy see nature again, take moments to pause and breathe. I reminded Mommy how to be silly and laugh, and I gave her unconditional love. Besides all this, I helped Mommy remember Animal-Speak. She could now communicate with animals and had helped some already. Most importantly for us, we would be able to communicate with each other from over the Bridge.

"Bear?" I called to him. "I helped a few humans, but mainly Mommy. I feel proud of my life, and I do believe I fulfilled my purpose."

Bear nodded. "Very good. You have learned an especially

important lesson. Life's Purpose does not have to be a huge spectacle or event. It is the little things that help others feel whole and loved that are most important. You reminded a human of who she was at her core. She is a Healer and was always a Healer. Now she needs to learn to trust herself and open her heart to another human," Bear said.

"Will she forget me?" I asked.

"There is no way your bond will ever be broken. You know this from when you were Wolf and she was your human then. Things change but remain the same," Bear said.

I knew Bear was right. Yet I still found myself sitting frozen at the end of the Bridge not wanting to move. I watched Mommy and Sister. I wished I could kiss them and make things better. Athena was patient. She watched me closely. I took a few steps closer to her side of the Bridge. Just a few steps. Not too far.

Behind Athena, I could see Roxie and her puppies. There were a lot of animals of every kind roaming around. They were all happy and joyful. The skies looked beautiful. The grass was green and vibrant. Green. I could see everything in color now! Wow! That was unexpected. I hadn't remembered that from my other transitions. I couldn't take my eyes off the land across the Bridge. The flowers were so vibrant. All the animals made happy sounds. There were so many, but it was not noisy or crowded.

Everything sounded like a beautiful song. All the beings got along, and there was such a feeling of peace and love. I looked at Athena, still waiting for me. She wagged her tail. I gave a little wag in response. Still, I looked back at the front of the Bridge, now behind me. When I looked over there, it felt heavy. I did not see colors. Everything looked gray. But there were Mommy and Sister, alone. Why couldn't they come with me? I knew the answer. I knew they couldn't. It was more wishful thinking again. I knew this.

So, if I was right, and I fulfilled my purpose, why did I still feel like I left something unfinished? I thought there was something else that I needed to do. I sat down on the Bridge, still hesitant to fully cross over, glancing one way and then the other. There was still more I had to do. I could *feel* it. I put my head down and rested, listening to Mommy's messages. Poor Mommy. *I'm here. I'm still here. Sort of. . .*

42

TRANSITIONING

 $\mathcal{I}$ visited Mommy all the time. I lay by her stomach and tried to ease the pain she felt inside. I saw her smiling gently sometimes. She knew I was there. Good. She was using her Animal-Speak more, and that was important. When Mommy was asleep, it was easier to send messages. I showed her things from our life together, and that made her happy. When she woke from sleep, she was sad to find me not there.

I took a few more steps toward Athena. I could see behind her. It really did look so amazing. I stood still and lifted my nose in the air to get more scents. Everything smelled clean and fresh and fragrant. So beautiful! Athena was wagging her tail. She was excited for me to move forward. I took a few more steps and then stopped. I was still on the Bridge; I kept moving forward toward Athena and then back again to the middle.

Mommy saw me standing in the middle of the bridge. She was happy to see me but also sad that I was not moving forward.

"It's okay, Baby! Go to Athena. She will show you what to do," Mommy said.

"I don't want to leave you. I want to come back home. I want to be with you!" I told her.

This was true. I did want to be home. I was not a young

soul, however, and knew this wasn't how it worked. I felt a pull toward Mommy still. I really did love being with her. But I also wanted to move forward. I still felt stuck. Change is hard, even for me. I took a few steps back toward the end.

"Maybe you can come here with me. It looks beautiful," I said excitedly, knowing that it wasn't possible but hopeful, nonetheless. Inside of me, I knew this was a selfish, horrible thought. For Mommy to come with me, that would mean she would lose her life. I did not want that at all. Struggles of the heart. That is what this was about.

"No, sweetheart. It isn't my time. We will be together soon. Remember, time moves differently there. It won't seem awfully long to you." Mommy said these words bravely, even though I knew she was sad and scared.

Mommy was very smart. Time did move differently. Still, I was struggling.

I took a deep breath and moved across the bridge. Athena stood up and was excited for me. I moved closer to her. I started walking faster. With each step, I felt lighter, stronger, and happier. I crossed the Bridge and was now with Athena and so many others. I turned around briefly looking back.

"I love you, Mommy! I will be here when you are ready."

Just that quickly, I transitioned. I was back Home. Home. The place all beings called Joy.

I spent time walking around with Athena. She walked me around and showed me everything. With each step, I began to remember it all. Athena and I talked about Mommy. We shared stories, and it helped me to know there were others that loved Mommy as much as I do. I met many old friends. The reunions were wonderful. I met new friends, too. Some of the new friends were different animals, animals Mommy helped along the way.

One friend is called Liz. She is an elephant. I remembered Mommy talking about "her" elephant. She helped feed Liz who lived on a Sanctuary. Liz lifted me up to her back with her trunk. I stood tall on her back and could see far across the land.

Everything was so incredible. I called out to Mommy hoping that she would see me with Liz.

I sent her a message saying, "Look! I am a mountain goat!" That was a little joke between me and Mommy that I hoped she would remember. I walked with Liz for a while then jumped off her back to run around and play. I was always a fast runner in Life, but now I was incredibly fast! I could leap higher than ever too. The water from the streams tasted delicious, so much better than the rain puddles in Life. All of us here always had full bellies, but we did not kill anything for food. We were just full and satisfied. Everyone was safe here. Even though we didn't get tired, I slept next to Athena. She let me curl up near her belly and put her paw around me. It reminded me of Mommy.

I talked to Mommy while she was sleeping. I showed her everything I was experiencing. I described everything and told her I felt much better. I was no longer in pain. I felt vibrant. I told Mommy that I could see colors. I told her about all the animals, including Wolf. I talked to Mommy nonstop, hoping she would hear all my messages. I told her how much I loved her and still love her. I promised I would never leave her. Even though we could not feel each other's physical bodies, I would always be with her.

When Mommy woke up, she was not so terribly sad. She felt a little better, a little less distraught. Mommy was slowly transitioning into her new life too.

43

JOY

I want to tell you more about Joy, because it is the most beautiful place in the Universe. As mentioned earlier, every Being is safe. There are animals of every kind here, but none of us hurts another. We all live harmoniously. Our bellies are full, so we do not need to eat. Sometimes, we will eat something that nature provides just for the taste, but we never kill another being. This reminded me of Mommy. Mommy stopped eating animals and animal products a while ago. She said it was difficult for her to eat Beings when she heard them. She also felt much healthier when she made that switch.

Joy had hills, mountains, prairies, canyons, everything you could possibly imagine. All the trees and plants were vibrant and healthy. Flowers had the most beautiful aroma. Nothing ever died here. Everything remained perfect. We never tired, but some of us liked to nap or just lie down and enjoy the beauty and company of others. I loved to stay close to Athena during these times. Roxie loved to stay with her puppies, and they were happy about that too. Most of the animals found their pack or friends from Life, and the celebrations were always fun. There were some animals that never had another animal friend. Athena and the other Greeters made sure they were introduced to others, and quickly they formed unions and friendships. No one ever felt lonely or alone here.

There were humans here too. The humans lived in the center of Joy. They were reunited with everyone special in their life! The animals could roam freely between the outside and the inside circle to visit humans. When I remembered this, I went to the middle to look for Grandma. I found her almost immediately. She had been watching and waiting for me to come to her. I was so happy to see her! She was healthy and happy and met a lot of friends and family members. Grandma liked to play music for everyone. She was talented, and everyone had such a great time. There were some family members that knew who I was, but I had never met them. Grandma had been talking about me to everyone. Everyone was waiting to greet me. I was still special!

I had a special friend in JOY—Squirrel! He followed me around until I recognized him. We laughed about how silly we were in Life. His chatter is not annoying anymore. We have a great time together. Sometimes he sits on my back while I run fast through the fields. He holds onto my scruff with his little hands. He likes when I run fast. I get it! I like to sit on top of Liz. It is so much fun. Sometimes I sit on Liz, and Squirrel sits on me! We are a tower of friends roaming through the fields. We all laugh inside and have a great time.

The beauty of Joy does not change my missing Mommy, but it does ease the pain. I no longer have regrets or any desire to go back; now, I look forward to when Mommy can live here with all of us. That won't be for a while though. She has other things to accomplish.

I spotted Wolf in the distance. It is weird to see your other self in person, but that is how it is. Wolf is with the ancients, the elders. He can come to the outside if he wants, but he mainly stays with his humans and pack. I did visit him though. We went nose to nose and licked faces. It felt great to see him, and I thanked him for showing me the way on so many occasions. Manners are still important, after all!

There is one more reunion that I want to share. Mom. When Mom saw me, she came running to me with great excitement. We nuzzled and jumped all over each other. She told me how proud she was of me. We snuggled together for a long time. It was so great to be near Mom again. I told her all about my life, even though she already knew. She had been watching me grow.

44

STILL CONNECTED

I talk to Mommy a lot. She doesn't always hear me the moment that I speak, but she hears me. I hear her all the time. She is sad without me but finds ways to manage. Sometimes I send her little gifts. The easiest gifts to send are little white butterflies. They flutter around near her when she is sitting outside. Mommy smiles. She knows they are from me. I make sure the Blue Jays and Red Cardinals fly close to her so she can see them. Grandma and I send those together. It's our "thing." Those and Hummingbirds. Grandma really loves hummingbirds. I also sent her a rabbit. I told the rabbit to look right at her. He didn't move at all, just stared at her. When she went close to him, he scampered away but walked to where I used to smell around in the bushes by the side of the house. Mommy looked at him from the deck. The rabbit looked up and just sat there looking at her. Mommy tossed down some carrot pieces. She understands that the rabbit is my gift. This makes me happy.

I also like to play little tricks to remind her that I am present. Mommy used to leave the music on for me when she went to work. She doesn't do that anymore; instead, before she leaves the house, she says, "Alexa, stop." The music stops. Sometimes, after Alexa stops, I make the music turn back on. Mommy stops and looks at Alexa and says, "Okay, Little Bear. You can listen to music today!" I see her teeth. She is happy with my trick.

I talk to Coqui sometimes too. I ask her to look after Mommy and Sister. Mommy told me that she lets Coqui come upstairs sometimes. She does not stay long, but it brings Mommy joy to have her upstairs. Coqui is starting to use Animal-Speak with Mommy. She shows Mommy love when she sees her. Sometimes, I ask Coqui to give Mommy extra kisses from me. I can see she does this. Coqui is a good friend.

My best gifts for Mommy take place while she is sleeping. I send her many messages and we talk freely. I love these moments. I show her things and remind her of things we used to do. Mommy laughs at the memories. I love hearing her laugh! Mommy tells me about her day, and I gladly listen. She tells me about Sister and Brother, too. She said Brother was sad about my crossing over. Sister is very sad too. Like Mommy, she is learning to adjust. Mommy says Sister sends her pictures of me while she is at work. That tells me and Mommy that I am still on her mind. I am very happy we took so many pictures and videos. It brings them joy to look at them now. Occasionally, Mommy is worried about something, human things. I fill her mind and heart with my presence and let her feel safe and loved. She knows I am there.

She calls out, "I love you, Little Bear!" and kisses the pillow of me that she keeps on the bed.

"I love you too, Mommy! So very much! I love you for always," I tell her in return.

45

MY PURPOSE

*M*ommy calls to me and asks for help. Brother is going to do something for work that is dangerous. Mommy is very worried. She asks me to protect him and to guide him. This moment is so powerful. It means that Mommy fully understands Life after Life. She understands that life is fluid and multidimensional; she understands there is no death, only change. Life continues after physical death in a different place, but it is only a thought away.

I suddenly understand my true purpose. It is what it always has been: Protector, Warrior, Soldier! YES! I. AM. WOLF. I am so excited and, of course, agree to help Brother. I start running around gathering sticks and logs. I am piling them up. I move quickly. I'm excited to be helpful! I gather leaves and twigs, but also big branches. You see? I was training for this moment my entire life!

Mommy asks what I am doing.

"I'm building a bonfire!" I say.

Mommy seems confused.

"Brother can't hear me, but he will see the light from this bonfire, and I will be able to lead him to safety!"

The bonfire will also help me protect Brother, Sister, and

Mommy from other dangers. With the light shining so brightly, I can call other helpers, both here and on earth. Mommy is so excited to hear this. She feels better about Brother's job; actually, she knows that no harm will come to him.

"What a smart, brave, good Little Bear you are!" Mommy says. "Thank you, Sweetheart!"

I am overjoyed. I have never felt so complete and satisfied. Athena and Roxie wag their tails at me. I get busy working. I will be ready whenever I am needed. I hear Bear's voice calling to me.

"You see, Little One? All things led to this moment. Everything you did on earth prepared you for this. You had to leave your life so that you could help your brother from the other side. You did very well teaching your human Animal-Speak, and now you can work together to help others in need. I am so proud of you," Bear says.

That makes me so happy! Bear is proud of me! Mommy loves me and can rely on me! As Bear always says: "It will be what it is meant to be." Yes! I am meant to be my humans' protector, guardian, companion, and friend. It doesn't matter where we are, we are connected. I will always be available to help! I *am* fulfilling my life's purpose.

Everything will be fine. I am on the job!

"I love you, Mommy. Someday I will be able to kiss your face and snuggle with you again. We will run around and play, lie on the grass, go for long walks, and enjoy each other's company. But not now, not yet. You still have work to do and your Purpose to fulfill. Stay true to your heart. Practice Animal-Speak. Let your guard down and trust love. Most importantly, remember, I am always with you. We are forever connected."

Life's Purpose. We all have one. Everything we experience, good or bad, prepares us for our unique purpose. It may not seem important, but every action affects another life. We are *all* connected.

Enjoy your life, embrace the little moments, and learn to

recognize your worth. Every Life has value and purpose! What is your purpose? Enjoy your Journey!

"I love you forever, Mommy. No amount of time or space will break our bond."
"Yes, Little One. I love you forever, too!" Mommy says, while listening to "A Song for You" by Leon Russell on Alexa. There really is a song for everything!

THE END
(Or the beginning!)

A PLACE CALLED JOY

BY DANIELA AMATO

There is a place across the bridge
All animals call Joy
There is no pain, fear, or loneliness
Just love, happiness, and joy.

The humans there were once in Life
Rewarded with endless days
Of snuggles, play, and happiness
Eternal Joy – in all ways.

The abused, neglected, and mistreated
Remember not their pain.
Finally, free of everything
That represents a chain.

With bellies full and gentle hands
Love is every Being's gain.

Forever in the land of Joy
All Beings feel the peace
The moment they touch the sacred ground
They experience caprice.

Someday I hope to cross the Bridge
that leads me to great Joy.
I'll feel the love and happiness
Of all who gave me joy.

Until that day, I'll carry on
In my heart you will remain
Reminding me of our great love,
Comforting till we meet again.

Then someday. . .
I'll know it's time
I'll hear your call
I'll see your face. . .

Greeting me with happiness
At the Rainbow Bridge that leads to Joy.

AFTERWORD

I cannot stress enough the beauty of Joy. This is the best place ever! Don't get me wrong, though. I have a lot of things to do. I have joined Athena as one of the Greeters. We have been busy, with the all the fires and natural disasters happening lately. I have been introduced to many new animals—Koalas, Kangaroos, Wallabies and more! Each are so grateful to enter Joy.

I am never too busy to help Mommy, though. Sometimes she needs help communicating with animals, and I talk to them and let them know that she is okay to speak with. It is a lot of fun working together! One of our last big jobs was helping a group of horses cross over. There was an accident. A terrible one. Mommy was on one end talking to them and giving comfort, and I was waiting anxiously on the other to show them the way. An amazing thing happened at that point. A beautiful glowing white Horse appeared next to me. She called them to her, and they followed. While all horses are beautiful, Spirit Horse was the most beautiful I have ever seen. She acknowledged me with her head, bending down so our foreheads touched. I was honored and felt special.

AFTERWORD

Working with Mommy has been wonderful. It makes the time we are physically separated easier. We are still connected. That is the most important part for Mommy too.

ABOUT THE AUTHOR

Daniela Amato was born in Italy and raised in the Bronx, New York. Growing up, Daniela was always fascinated with all things related to animals. Visiting zoos and aquariums was always a double–edged sword. She loved to see the animals but hated that they were not free to roam as nature intended.

Daniela spent hours alone pretending and cultivating her creative side and imagination. She often imagined the animals were speaking to her. It was not until later in life that Daniela realized it was not her imagination; the animals were, in fact, communicating with her through picture messages and energy.

Currently a massage therapist, business owner, author, and mother of two grown children, Daniela's love for animals and nature continues to grow. Because of this love and respect, Daniela has chosen a plant–based lifestyle. "It is hard to eat someone when you can hear them talk to you," she says. This lifestyle prompted Daniela to write her first book *If it Was Me. . . A Child's Journey Through Reflection*. The book is beautifully illustrated by artist Carlos Franco and explores the relationship between the animals we love to see and the food on our plates. Gently told, *If it Was Me* is an emblem for compassion, empathy, and love toward all beings.

Animal-Speak, or animal communication, is a practice that has brought great joy and occasional sadness. It is a gift and a curse; but, with love and compassion, Daniela focuses on the positive and treats it as a Gift from the Universe. Daniela currently helps others communicate with animals here and beyond. For more information, visit www.danielaamato.com or contact her directly at animalconnections11@gmail.com

"There is a lot we can learn from our animal friends. Their wisdom goes beyond what humans seem capable or willing to embrace. Animals hold on to the primal gifts of the Universe; learning Animal-Speak has helped me reconnect with those natural instincts and understand Nature better. Not every message is life-changing; however, for the animal sending the message it is important." Daniela believes if humans learned to hear with their hearts and not their minds, we would be able to resolve many of the issues society faces.

CPSIA information can be obtained
at www.ICGtesting.com
Printed in the USA
BVHW032134171120
593603BV00019B/136